Blues Guitar
for adults

The Grown-Up Approach to Playing Blues Guitar

WAYNE RIKER

Recorded at Standing Room Only, Fontana, CA

Cover Photo: BP&V Photographic Associates
Fender guitar courtesy of The Joe Bouchard Collection
Special thanks to Leo Valcourt and Louisette Bolduc for the use of their home.

Alfred Music Publishing Co., Inc.
P.O. Box 10003
Van Nuys, CA 91410-0003
alfred.com

ISBN-10: 0-7390-9287-1 (Book & CD)
ISBN-13: 978-0-7390-9287-3 (Book & CD)

Contents

About the Author.. 4
Introduction 5
Reading Music: A Quick Review 6
Reading Tablature (TAB): A Quick Review 8
Common Chords 10

Chapter One: The Twelve-Bar Blues Format   11

Chapter Two: The Eight-Bar Blues Format   20

Chapter Three: Blues Techniques   24

Hammer-Ons 24
Pull-Offs.. 25
The Finger Slide 26
The Trill 27
Bending 28
Bend & Vibrato 30
Pre-Bends—The Crying Bend Sound 30
Release Bends 31

Chapter Four: Basic Improvisation   34

The Blues Scale 34
Thinking Outside the Box 35
Pentatonic Scales 36

Chapter Five: Minor Blues   42

Natural Minor Scales 44

Chapter Six: Arpeggios   46

Dominant 7 Arpeggios...................................... 46
Minor 7 Arpeggios 50

Chapter Seven: Improvising Over
I7–IV7–V7 in E   54

Twelve-Bar Blues Solo in E................................ 55
Licks in the Style of Freddie King...................... 56

Chapter Eight: Improvising Over
I7–IV7–V7 in A   58

Twelve-Bar Blues Solo in A 59
Licks in the Style of Mike Bloomfield 60

Chapter Nine: Improvising Over
I7–IV7–V7 in G   62

Twelve-Bar Blues Solo in G 63
Licks in the Style of Eric Clapton...................... 64

Chapter Ten: Improvising Over
I7–IV7–V7 in C 66

Twelve-Bar Blues Solo in C 67
Licks in the Style of Muddy Waters 68

Chapter Eleven: Improvising Over
i7–iv7–v7 in A Minor 70

Twelve-Bar Blues Solo in A Minor 71
Licks in the Style of Albert King 72

Chapter Twelve: Improvising Over
i7–iv7–v7 in E Minor 74

Twelve-Bar Blues Solo in E Minor 75
Licks in the Style of Robert Cray 76

Chapter Thirteen: Improvising Over
Gospel Blues Changes in D 78

Eight-Bar Blues Solo in D 79
Licks in the Style of B. B. King 80

Chapter Fourteen: Improvising Over
Gospel Blues Changes in A 82

Eight-Bar Gospel Blues Solo in A 83
Licks in the Style of Otis Rush 84

Chapter Fifteen: Improvising Over a Blues
in the Style of "Stormy Monday" 86

Twelve-Bar Stormy Solo in G 87
Licks in the Style of T-Bone Walker 88

Chapter Sixteen: Improvising Over
Alternate Blues Changes in B♭ 90

Solo Over Alternate Twelve-Bar Blues
Changes in B♭ 91
Licks in the Style of Tiny Grimes 92

Scales...94
Arpeggios 96

Track
1

A compact disc is available for this book. This disc can make learning with the book easier and more enjoyable. The symbol shown above appears next to every example that is on the CD. Use the CD to help ensure that you are capturing the feel of the examples, interpreting the rhythms correctly, and so on. All the full-length solos include a live band and opportunities for you to jam along. The track numbers below the symbols correspond to the examples you want to hear. Track 1 will help you tune your guitar to this CD.

Have fun!

Contents

About the Author

Wayne Riker has been a guitar teacher and performer since 1970, playing and teaching all styles of music. A graduate of the Guitar Institute of Technology (1980), Wayne has conducted and co-hosted blues workshops across the country, in addition to writing instructional columns for *Guitar Player*, *Acoustic Guitar*, and *Premier Guitar* magazines. Currently, he is a freelance guitarist and composer in the San Diego area, recording original instrumental tracks with his quintet, as well as solo acoustic guitar material. His two recent CDs, *Fretology* and *Penumbral Sky*, have received high acclaim.

For updates and contact information, please visit: www.waynerikerguitar.com

ACKNOWLEDGEMENTS
I would like to recognize some of the excellent musicians in Southern California whose influence and friendship have not been forgotten: Paul LaRose, Joe Diorio, Peter Sprague, Jeff Johnson, Chris Vitas, Phil Shopoff, Will Parsons, Fred Lanuza, Bill Doyle and Jody Fisher.

Introduction

This book is specifically designed for adult guitarists sweeping the cobwebs off their guitar cases or just looking for some blues inspiration. It assumes you already play and have tried your hand at the blues before. The first two chapters cover very basic rhythms and chord progressions that are paramount for playing the blues, either in a group or on your own.

In Chapters Three through Six, I have mapped out the necessary skills for soloing, including all the hand techniques that will embellish your licks and the nuts and bolts of scale and arpeggio theory for blues improvisation. A CD comes with this book. Listen to it and play along with all the musical examples.

Chapters Seven through Sixteen of this book are designed to give you new improvisational ideas in the classic blues idiom by studying solos over ten specific twelve- and eight-bar blues progressions in the styles of ten different blues guitarists. Hopefully, some are your heroes from the past and present. If you are uncertain about any scales or arpeggios listed, check the glossary in the Appendix on pages 94 and 95. Learn to play each solo at the suggested tempo and then transfer the improvisational ideas to similar situations. Also, catalogue the licks over the I7, IV7 and V7 chords and use them in your own playing style. Most great improvisers in every style of music learned their trade by carefully studying the way their predecessors played over each chord change.

Each chapter is laid out in the same fashion, opening with the chord structure we will be improvising over, followed by a brief discussion of the main aspects of the sample solo provided. Then we look at a short historical sketch of each guitarist, followed by six licks in their style. Match up these licks over each chapter's chord progression. This will help to add more vocabulary to the ideas demonstrated in each solo. Once again, make sure you listen to the CD for this book or, even better, recordings of these great artists to capture the spirit of each style. In particular, listen to the choking, vibrato and bending techniques that are so hard to represent on paper.

Have fun!

Reading Music
a quick review

 **Pitch**

Learning to read music will help you to get the most out of this book. It will make you a better musician, too, because you will be able to communicate more easily with other musicians. What follows is a quick review of music reading basics. If you don't need it, skip it. Remember that practice makes perfect! The more you practice reading, the easier it will become.

STAFF

A staff containing five lines and four spaces is used in the writing of music. Notes are alternately written on the lines and spaces in alphabetical order.

CLEF

The clef indicates which notes coincide with a particular line or space. Different clefs are used for different instruments. Guitar music is written in G clef. The inside curl of the G clef encircles the line which is called "G." When the G clef is placed on the second line, as in guitar music, it is called the *treble clef*.

Using the G clef, the notes are as follows:*

E G B D F F A C E G

LEDGER LINES

Ledger lines are lines that are used to indicate pitches above and below the staff.

Ledger lines

Ledger lines

E F G A B C D

A B C D E F G

* In standard notation the guitar sounds an octave lower than written.

Blues Guitar for Adults

 **Time**

THE MEASURE

The staff is divided by vertical lines called *bar lines*. The space between two bar lines is a *measure*. Each measure (bar) is an equal unit of time.

Double bar lines ☰ mark the end of a section or example.

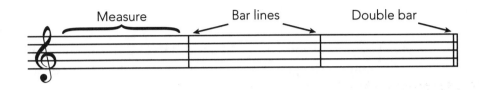

TIME SIGNATURE

Every piece of music has numbers at the beginning that tell us how to count the time.

The top number represents the number of beats or counts per measure. The bottom number represents the type of note receiving one count.

For example:
4 = quarter note   8 = eighth note

4 = Four beats per measure
4 = A quarter note ♩ equals one beat

Examples:

$$\frac{4}{4} \qquad \frac{3}{4} \qquad \frac{6}{4}$$

Sometimes a **C** is written in place of $\frac{4}{4}$ time. This is called *common time*.

NOTE & REST VALUES IN $\frac{4}{4}$ TIME

A whole note	𝅝	or rest ▬	= four beats
A half note	𝅗𝅥	or rest ▬	= two beats
A quarter note	♩	or rest 𝄽	= one beat
An eighth note	♪	or rest 𝄾	= ½ beat
A sixteenth note	𝅘𝅥𝅯	or rest 𝄿	= ¼ beat

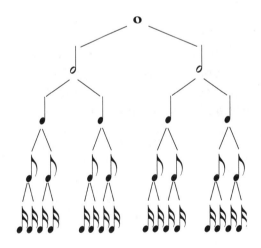

Notes shorter than a quarter note are usually beamed together in groups.

Eighths- - ¬ Sixteenths - -¬   Eighths - - - - - - - ¬

Reading Tablature (TAB)
a quick review

The combination of Tablature (TAB) and standard music notation provides the most complete system for communicating the many possibilities in guitar playing.

In the TAB used in this book, rhythm is not indicated. For that, you will have to refer to the standard notation. Six lines are used to indicate the six strings of the guitar. The top line is the high E string (the thinnest string, closest to the floor) and the bottom line is the low E string (the thickest string, closest to the ceiling). Numbers are placed on the strings to indicate frets. If there is a "0," play that string open.

Fingerings are often included in TAB. You will find them just under the bottom line. A "1" indicates your left index finger. A "2" indicates your left middle finger, and so on.

In the following example, the first note is played with the 1st finger on the 1st fret. The next note is played with the 2nd finger on the 2nd fret, the 3rd finger plays the 3rd fret and the 4th finger plays the 4th fret.

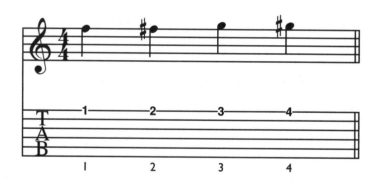

A *tie* in the music (a curved line that joins two or more notes of the same pitch into one longer note) is indicated in TAB by placing the tied note in parentheses.

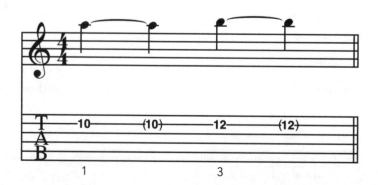

Blues Guitar for Adults

Hammer-ons (striking a string to sound a note with just the left hand) and *pull-offs* (pulling a left-hand finger off a string in such a way as to sound a note without plucking with the right hand) are indicated with *slur* marks, just like in standard notation. We also use an "H" for hammer-ons and a "P" for pull-offs. See pages 24 and 25 for more on these techniques. These are found just above the TAB.

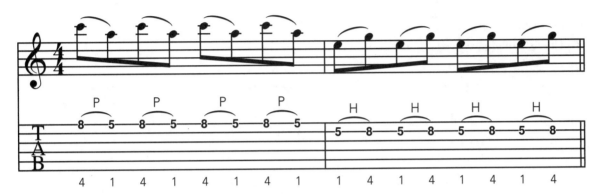

Upward bends (see page 28) are marked with upward arrows. Downward arrows are used to show a bend being released. A number above the arrow indicates how far to bend (1 = a whole step, ½ = a half step, etc.). Remember that the TAB will show the fret number on which your finger should be placed. The standard music notation shows the actual resulting sound. Notice that the small grace note in the standard notation corresponds with the fret shown in the TAB. In the following example, you will also find a tap (T) and a *slide* (S and ╱). Notice that if two or more notes are played with one bend, they appear in parentheses in the TAB. Some notes are actually represented by the arrows themselves, as in the second note of the triplet in this example.

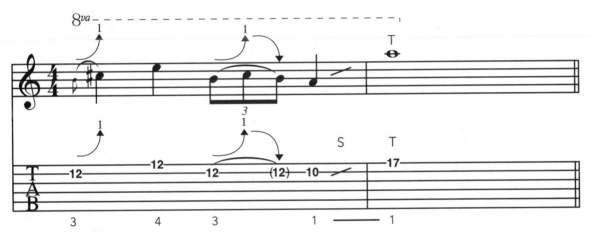

In the following example you will find several more symbols sometimes used in TAB. The sign for vibrato (〰), and the signs for picking down (⊓) and picking up (∨).

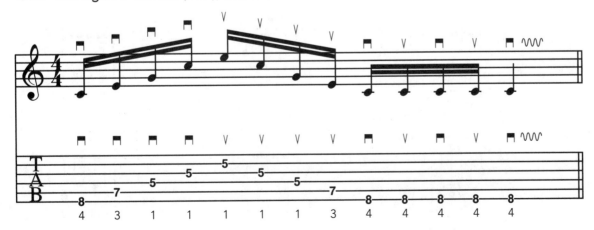

Reading Music: A Quick Review

Common Chords

Here is a glossary of the most common chord forms used throughout this book.

A7

A7

A9

Amin

Amin7

Amin7

B♭7

B7

B7

B9

Bmin

C

C7

C9

D

D/A

D7

Dmin7

D#dim7

E7

E7

E7#9

E9

EAug

Emin7

Emin7
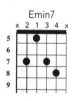

Fmin7

F#7

G

G/D

GMaj7

G#dim7

Blues Guitar for Adults

Chapter One
the twelve-bar blues format

Let's start by learning some classic *twelve-bar blues* rhythm patterns. This is the most basic blues form. As the name indicates, the form is twelve measures long. At its most basic level, it uses only three 7 chords. These are labeled with Roman numerals indicating their position in the key: I7(1), IV7(4) and V7(5). For example, in the key of C, I7 is C7, IV7 is F7 and V7 is G7 (C=1, D=2, E=3, F=4 and G=5). If you know the alphabet, you can figure out your I7(1), IV7(4) and V7(5) chords. Knowing your key signatures will also help. It is a good idea to pick up a theory book and at least learn the basics.

Lee McClenaghan, 50
College Professor

"I'm fulfilling a life-long ambition to perform publicly and have fun. This sure beats teaching college students all day."

To the right is the standard progression (succession or pattern of chords) for a twelve-bar blues. Each chord equals one measure. They are labeled 1 through 12 to help you see where each chord belongs in the form.

$I7_1$	$I7_2$	$I7_3$	$I7_4$
$IV7_5$	$IV7_6$	$I7_7$	$I7_8$
$V7_9$	$IV7_{10}$	$I7_{11}$	$V7_{12}$

We'll work in the most common blues guitar keys (E, A, G and C). These examples should help pull you out of the doldrums of just strumming dominant 7 chords. Memorize the I7(1), IV7(4) and V7(5) chords in each key as you learn the rhythms in the next six examples.

Below is a classic blues rhythm pattern in the key of E. The fingers moving above the open bass strings are playing an interval (the distance between two notes) of a 6th. Notice how the music in bars 11 and 12 makes you want to start from the beginning again. This is called a *turnaround*. Learn it and use it in other twelve-bar blues tunes in E.

NOTE

You'll find many examples in this book marked "Swing 8ths." In blues, it is common to *swing* the eighth notes. To swing the eighths, play the first note in each pair slightly longer and the second one shorter. The effect is similar to a triplet with the first two eighths tied.

Swing 8ths

Blues Guitar for Adults

This next pattern shows a great way to add bulk to a slow blues tune. The half-step (one-fret) finger-slide up and back down a whole step (two frets) mimics a common blues horn idea. Hit the chord shown as a small grace note directly on the beat and then immediately slide your hand up to the next chord and then down to the next. The dominant 9th chords (E9, A9 and B9—see page 10) create a full sound over slow blues patterns.

Chapter One: The Twelve-Bar Blues Format

This open-string, boogie-woogie-based rhythm works well for blues grooves in A. Notice that the same shape is played on different string sets over this I7–IV7–V7 progression.

Example 5 is a common blues *riff* or *motif* (a short repeated musical idea). It is the type commonly thought of as a bass line and is played between striking each chord in the progression. This riff will add lots of punch behind many a blues tune.

Make sure you know this next example well. It's the most typical *closed-position* (no open strings) formula for a blues shuffle. The stretch between the 3rd and 4th fingers on beats 2 and 4 of each bar may feel tough at first. Practice it for just a few minutes at a time until it becomes comfortable.

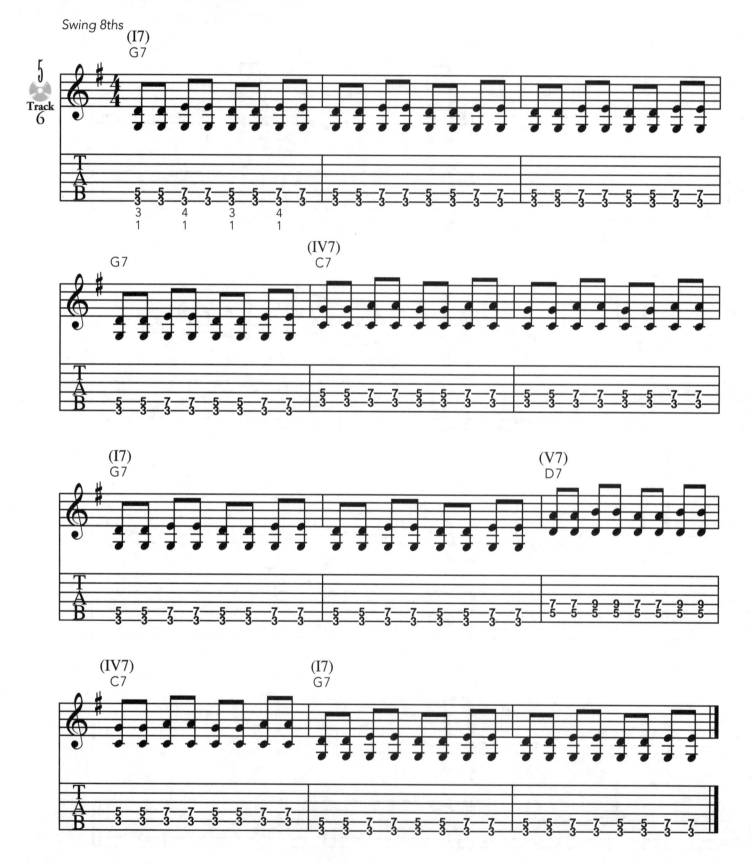

Here is a classic use of the interval of a 3rd in blues
rhythm playing. This rhythm would also work nicely
as a second guitar part in a two-guitar band.

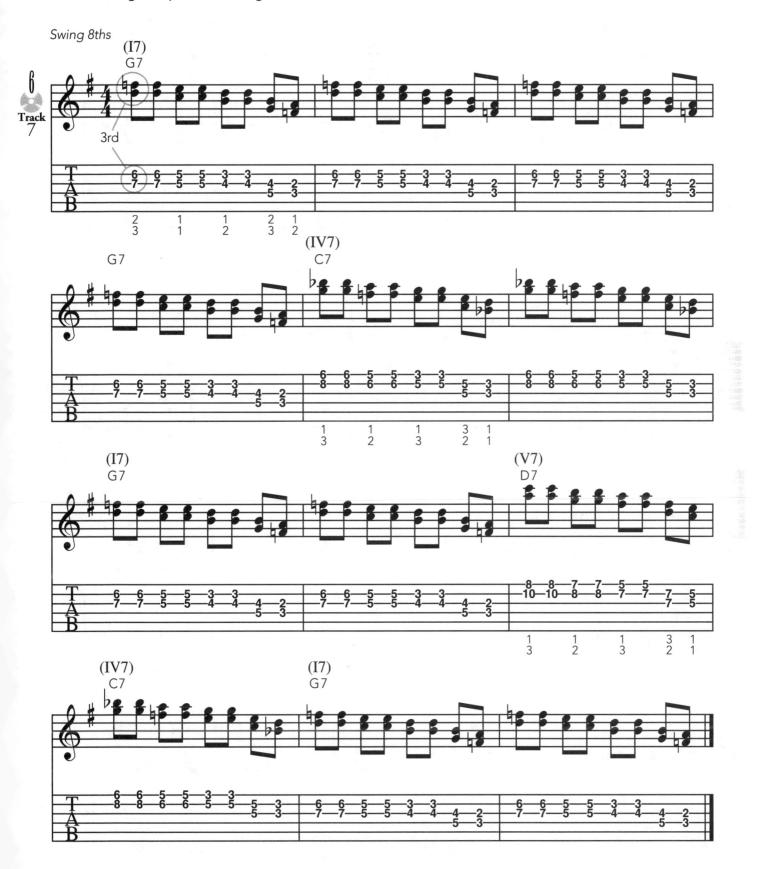

Once again, let's stretch those ligaments.
Keep your wrist low behind the neck as
the 4th finger reaches to the notes on
beats 2, 3 and 4.

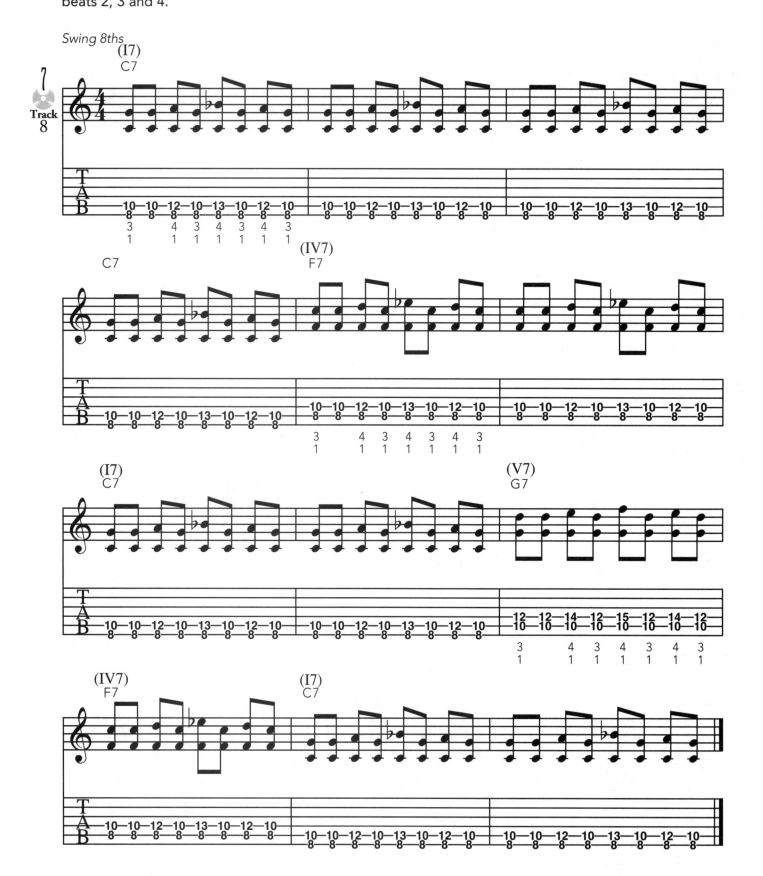

Track 9

NOTE

In this book, if a piece or example is *not* marked "Swing 8ths," it should be played with straight eighths.

This funky blues rhythm grooves with a hard-driving, single-note riff after each chord.

Chapter Two
the eight-bar blues format

In the next four examples, we will explore the *eight-bar blues* format. The eight-bar blues structure usually deviates from the twelve-bar pattern by the second bar. The twelve-bar blues will either remain on I or take a quick side trip to IV in bar 2, while the eight-bar blues usually proceeds to the V chord or the III7 chord in bar 2.

	Measure:	1	2		1	2
Twelve-bar blues:		I7	I7	or	I7	IV7
In G:		G7	G7		G7	C7
Eight-bar blues:		I7	V7	or	I7	III7
In G:		G7	D7		G7	B7

This first eight-bar blues example is a gospel-style blues progression in the key of D. Most gospel-blues tunes use *back-cycles of 5ths*. Back-cycling is analyzing chord motion from right to left. We look at the second of a pair of chords and relate the previous chord to it. For example, figuring from the A7 chord in bar 8, the previous chord, E, is V7. Figuring from the E, the chord before it, B7, is V7. Another common description for this kind of progression is "a cycle of 5ths." All the chords are five notes away from each other in the musical alphabet. Again, a basic knowledge of theory is helpful. There are many good books out there. Try, for example, *Theory for the Contemporary Guitarist* (16755).

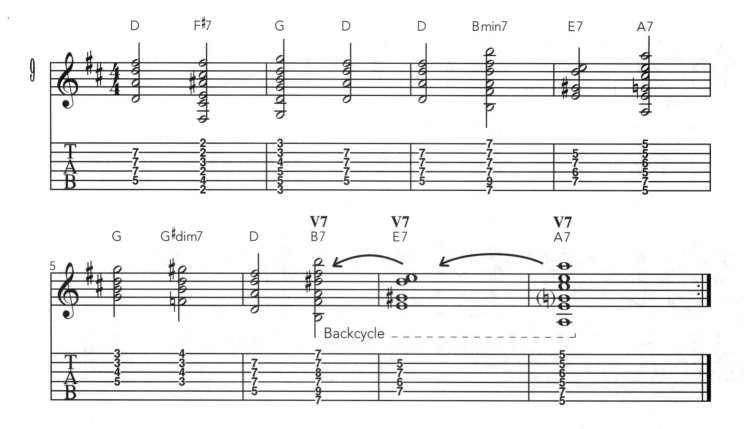

This example is in the style of the classic eight-bar Big Bill Broonzy tune, "Key to the Highway." Notice the appearance of the V chord in bar 2. This tune uses the same rhythm as example 6 on page 16.

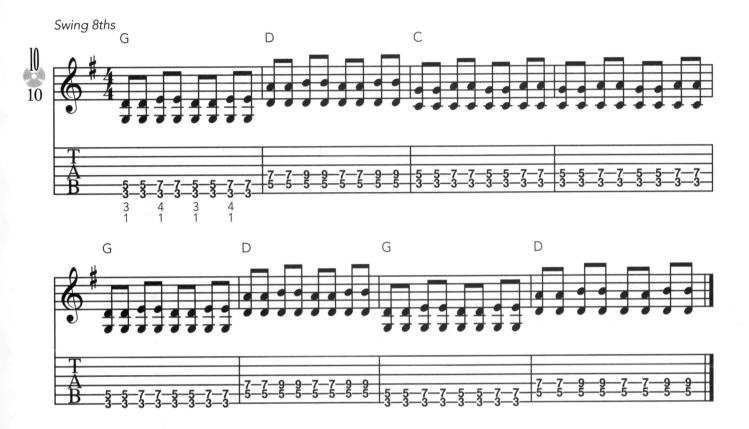

Alan Henry, 41
Civil Designer

"I was distracted by sports at a younger age, so I waited later in life to learn guitar. I'm totally hooked on it now. Of all the instruments to learn, guitar is the best!"

Chapter Two: The Eight-Bar Blues Format

Next is a traditional eight-bar minor-blues pattern. It has a distinctive chord structure. Notice that the first chord (Amin) is minor. It is indicated with a lower case Roman numeral (i). The V7 (E7) is the same but the IV chord (Dmin) is now minor (iv). Also distinctive is the inclusion of the VI chord, F.

This is in the style of the classic blues tune, "St. James Infirmary."

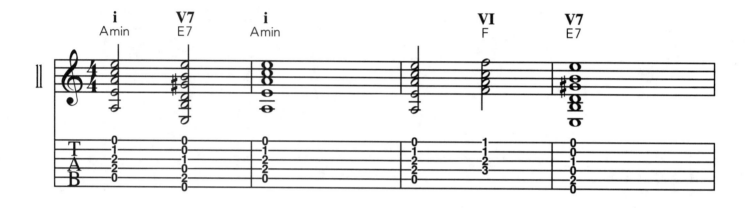

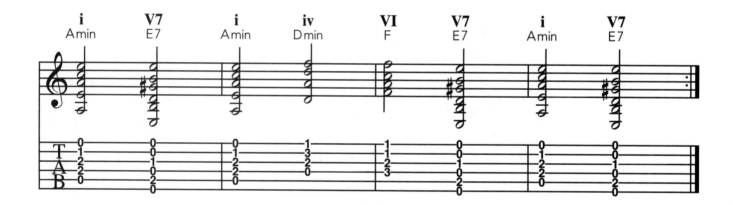

Blues Guitar for Adults

"It's great therapy from everyday stress. My wife challenged me to learn guitar. My goal is to play with other adults and accompany singers."

Steve Cyr, 45
Architect

Here's a minor blues in E:

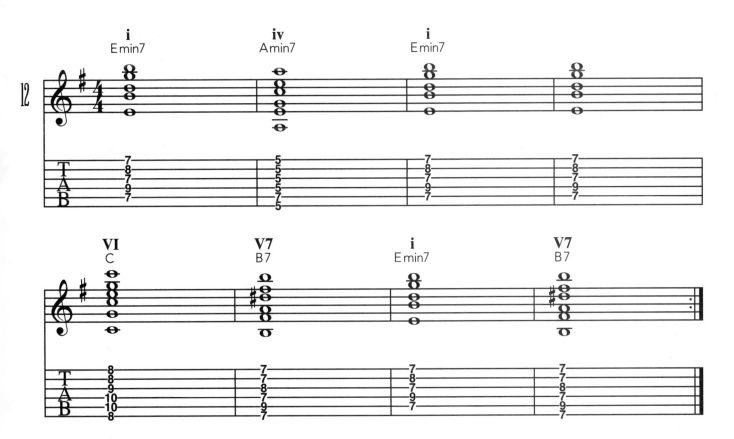

Chapter Three
blues techniques

The most important aspect of single-note blues technique is the emotional expression of each tone. This expressiveness is created through the use of hammer-ons, pull-offs, finger slides, trills, accurate bending, release bends, choking and vibrato. It is never too late to develop these skills. Enhancing these techniques should pave the way towards quality over quantity. In blues, we often strive to play less notes with more feeling.

 Hammer-Ons

Hammer-ons are executed by quickly dropping the finger on the string in such a way as to make a note or notes sound without picking the string with the right hand. Make sure the hammered notes sound. Notice the use of curved slur lines in the music and TAB, along with the "H" above the TAB to indicate the hammer-ons. Keep the rhythm of the notes even.

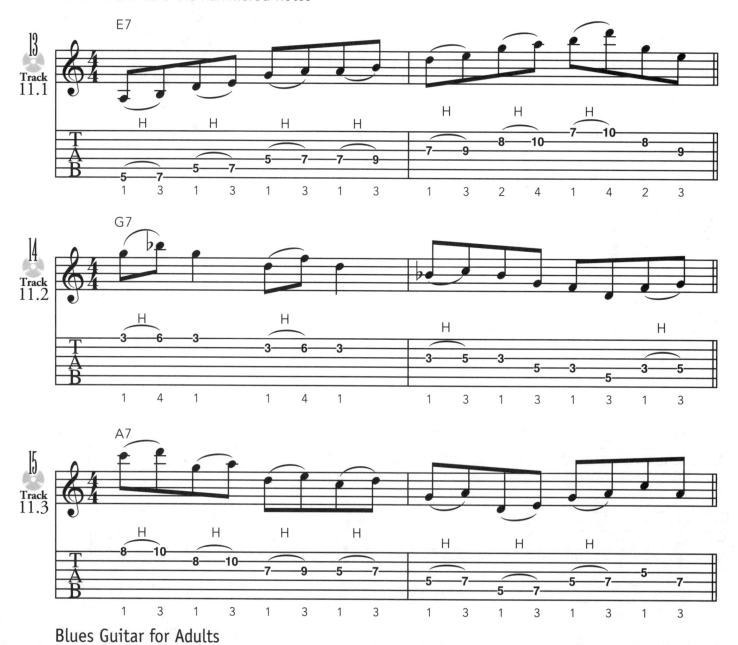

Pull-Offs

Make sure your finger is already down on the note you are pulling off to. The right hand picks only the first note under the slur. Pull the pull-off finger slightly down and away for the optimum pull-off sound. It's as if you are lightly plucking the string with the left hand. Note the use of the "P" above the TAB along with the slur lines to indicate this technique.

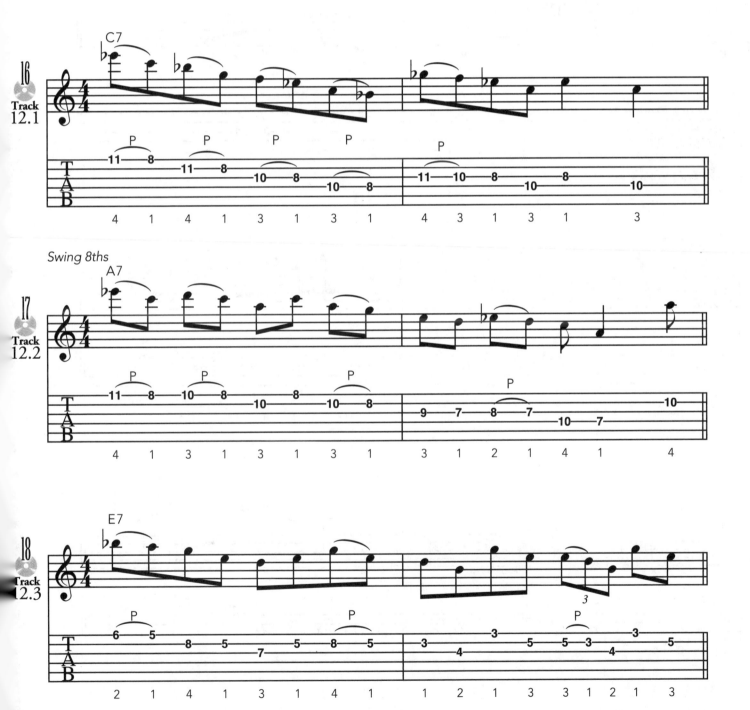

The Finger Slide

Just as with hammer-ons and pull-offs, only the first note in a slide is picked. Slide the finger directly to the desired fret while the string is still ringing from picking the first note to sound the second note. Keep your finger securely on the string as you slide to the next pitch and make sure you push your finger strongly on the destination fret. The note you slide to should be equally balanced in sound with the picked note. Notice the use of the slur lines and the "S" above the TAB to indicate slides. Also, notice that slides are usually written as small grace notes in the music. We play them directly on the beat and quickly move to the main note. The slide is like the vocal effect of *glissing* up (or down) to a note.

LESSON

S / = slide up
S \ = slide down

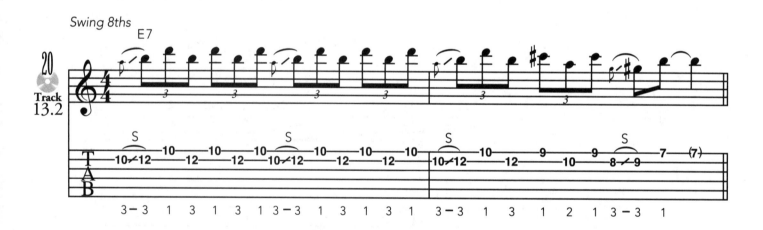

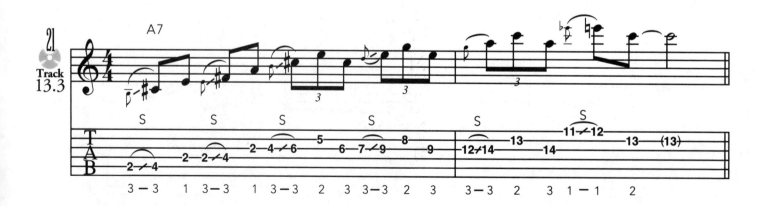

Blues Guitar for Adults

 **The Trill**

A *trill* is a hammer-on and pull-off combination which creates a rapid alternation between two notes. They are greatfinger exercises. Practice keeping the hammer-on and pull-off sounds as equal as possible. Each of the following examples uses trills with different combinations of half and whole steps.

LESSON

 = Trill between these notes for two beats (for the note value shown).

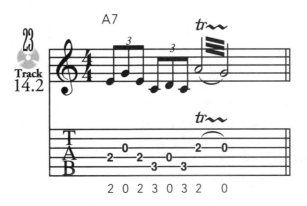

"At this time in my life, I have periods in my day when my children are at school. This is when I practice. I love to play for my children and my husband."

Maria Breen, 35
Wife and Mother

Chapter Three: Blues Techniques

 **Bending**

Bending the strings is at the heart of the blues sound. Like the finger slides, bends create a very vocal sound imitating the way singers will slide between notes in a way many instruments cannot.

To bend, put your 3rd finger on the starting pitch, pick the string and push the string up towards the ceiling. For the best control of your bends, make sure your 1st, 2nd and 3rd fingers are glued together as one bending mechanism. The following examples take you through bending different intervals. *Choke* (stop) the note after it reaches its intended pitch. Test your bends by first playing the destination pitch of the bend and then matching that pitch with a bend. For example, play a B♭ on the 6th fret of the 1st string, then bend the 5th fret A up one half step so that it sounds like the B♭ on the 6th fret. This is how we develop accurate bends.

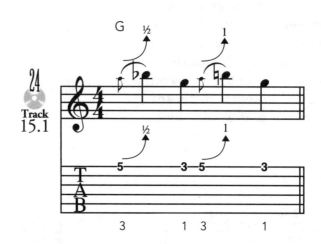

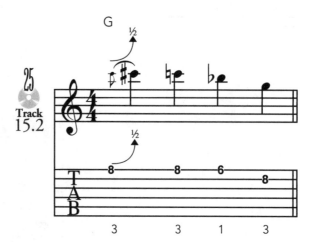

½	= half-step bend (one fret).
1	= whole-step bend (two frets).
1½	= whole-plus-half-step bend (three frets).

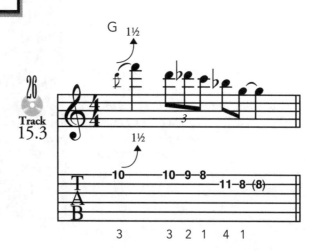

Blues Guitar for Adults

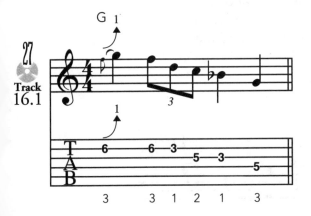

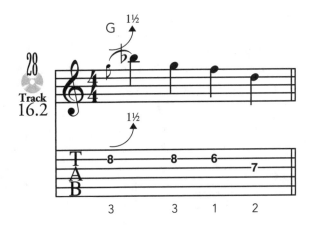

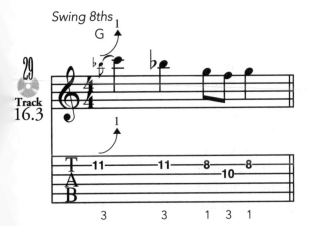

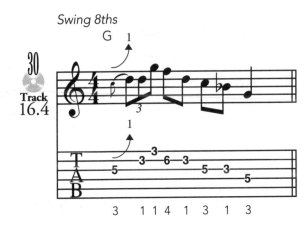

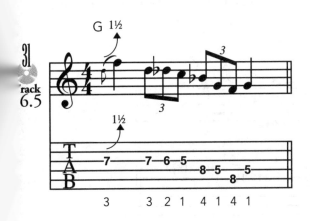

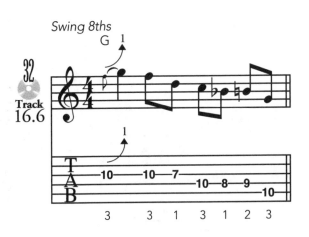

Chapter Three: Blues Techniques

Bend & Vibrato

Vibrato is yet another way the guitar imitates the human voice. Only choir boys sing with a pure, unaffected sound. Almost always, singers add life and emotion to their melodies with a subtle wavering of pitch that we call vibrato. In the next four exercises, practice bending to the intended pitch and then shaking the note back and forth in an up (towards the ceiling) and down (towards the floor) motion; this creates vibrato. You should feel your wrist and forearm helping the rocking vibrato motion. Listen to B.B. King—the master of vibrato. Practice the vibrato at slow, medium and fast speeds and try maintaining an even vibrato throughout the duration of the affected note.

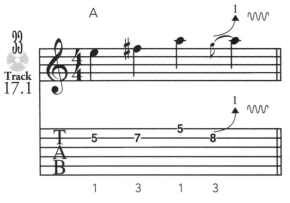

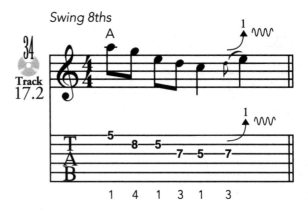

Pre-Bends— The Crying Bend Sound

After you've had some experience bending notes, you can start to estimate how far to bend a string for a whole- or a half-step bend. If you bend first, then pick the string, you can hear the note glide downward as you release the string to its unbent position. This is called a *pre-bend*. The effect is a very emotional, crying sound, sometimes called a swell.

The notes to be pre-bent are shown in parentheses with an arrow pointing straight up. A downward arrow shows the crying, release sound. In the first example below, the F on the 10th fret of the 3rd string is pre-bent up to sound like a G. The note is then picked and we listen as the bend releases to the F before playing the E♭.

HERE'S A TIP...

For an even better crying effect, use your volume control or a volume pedal to cut your sound while you pick, then bring your sound up as the note releases. We will know you most defintely have the blues!

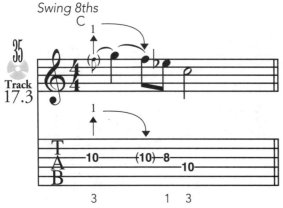

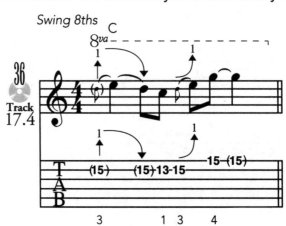

Blues Guitar for Adults

Release Bends

Release bends are almost self-explanatory. After you have initiated the bend, let the bent note drop back down to the starting point of the bend without picking. This is shown with a combination of up and down arrows. Dig into the wood to produce an even release. Play carefully through the following examples. Some of them are combined with regular choked bends.

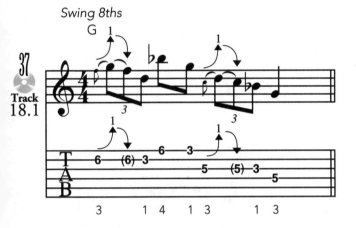

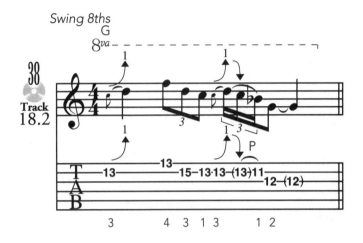

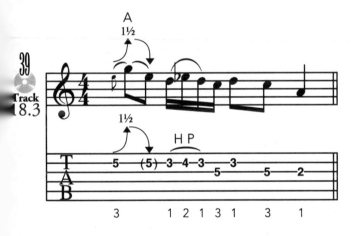

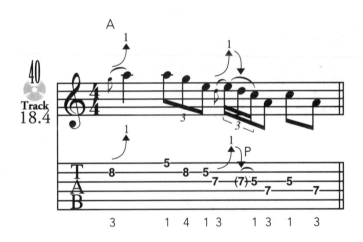

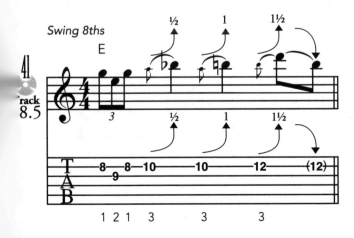

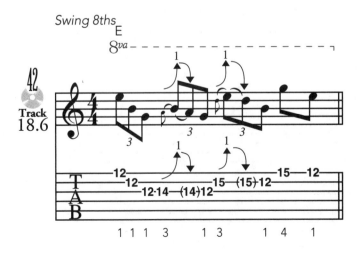

Chapter Three: Blues Techniques

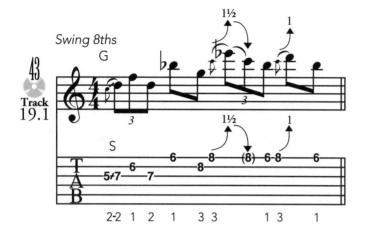

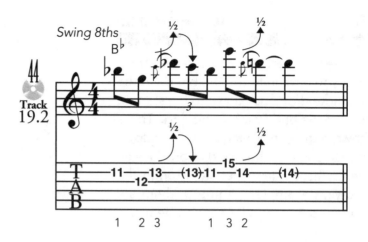

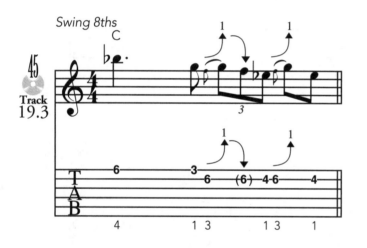

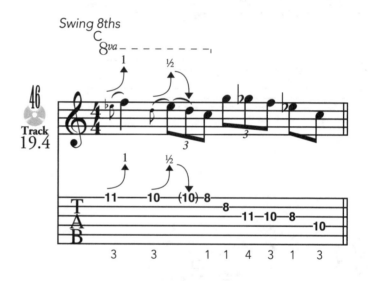

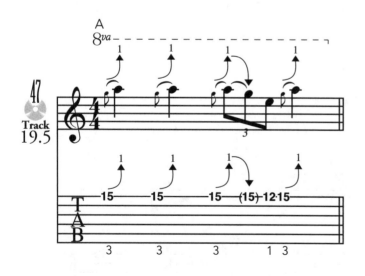

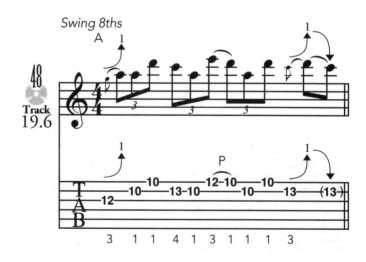

Blues Guitar for Adults

The next two examples feature lower-string bending technique. In each example, bend the string downward (toward the floor).

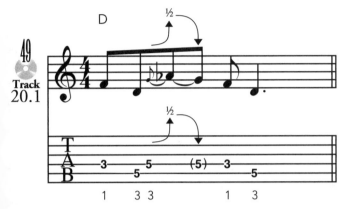

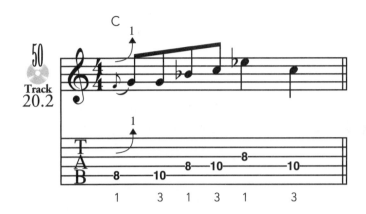

Let's combine techniques. Connect a slide into a bend and release. Pick the initial note of the slide and don't pick again until the note after the bend and release.

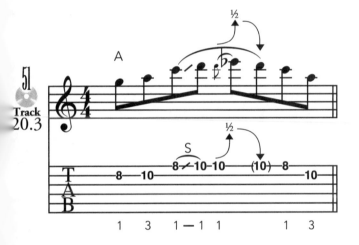

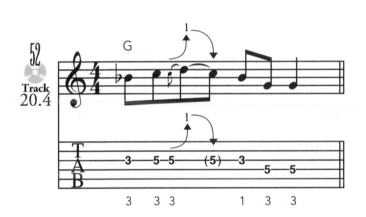

Connect a hammer-on and pull-off, respectively, into bends.

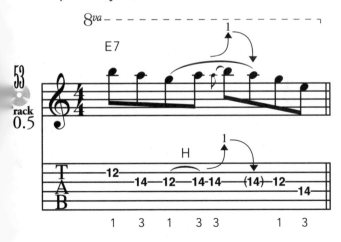

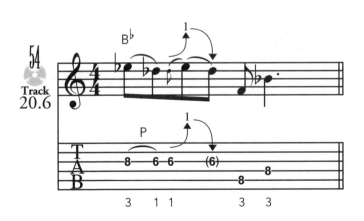

Chapter Three: Blues Techniques

Chapter Four
basic improvisation

 **The Blues Scale**

Blues players tend to think in terms of scales. The most commonly used scale is the *blues scale*. Learn the five patterns below in the keys of E and A. All these patterns are fully transposable to all other keys. If you know where the root appears in each scale and you know where the notes fall on the guitar, you can move any one of the patterns to any root you like.

The best way of thinking about a scale is with scale *degree* numbers. The notes of a major scale are numbered 1 through 8. For example, a C Major scale would be C=1, D=2, E=3, F=4, G=5, A=6, B=7, C=8 (major scales always have a half step between 3 and 4 and 7 and 8). The notes of the blues scale include some alterations of the major scale: 1 (root)–♭3–4–♭5–5–♭7. So the C Blues scale would be: C=1, E♭=♭3, F=4, G♭=♭5, G=5, B♭=♭7.

Learn these "box" patterns that move "vertically" across the strings.

The E Blues Scale	E – G – A – B♭ – B – D
	1 – ♭3 – 4 – ♭5 – 5 – ♭7

Pattern #1

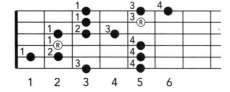

Pattern #2

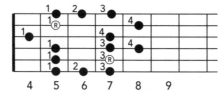

Pattern #3

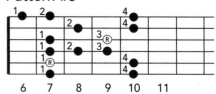

Pattern #4

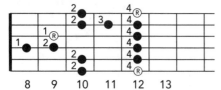

Pattern #5

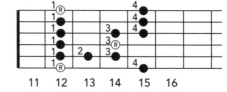

The A Blues Scale	A – C – D – E♭ – E – G
	1 – ♭3 – 4 – ♭5 – 5 – ♭7

Pattern #1

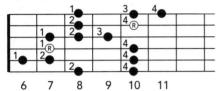

6   7   8   9   10   11

Pattern #2

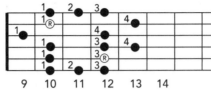

9   10   11   12   13   14

Pattern #3

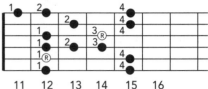

11   12   13   14   15   16

Pattern #4

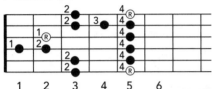

1   2   3   4   5   6

Pattern #5

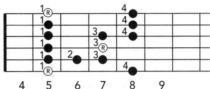

4   5   6   7   8   9

Thinking Outside the Box

Now that you have learned the blues scale patterns, let's look at the two most common blues scale patterns moving in a lateral (horizontal) motion across the neck. Once again, these patterns are fully transposable to all other keys. Many blues players often use these lateral patterns. They are really just a combination of parts of the vertical scale patterns or "boxes" you learned on page 34. The more familiar you are with those, the easier it is to combine them. Combining them creates a much more fluid playing style. You don't want to get "stuck in the boxes."

E BLUES SCALE

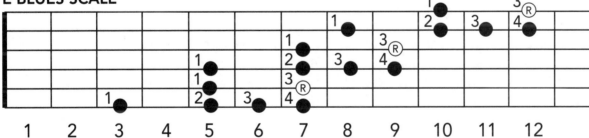

1   2   3   4   5   6   7   8   9   10   11   12

A BLUES SCALE

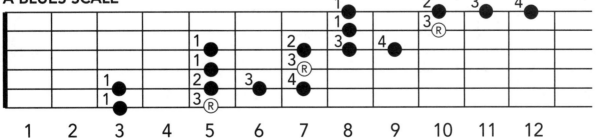

1   2   3   4   5   6   7   8   9   10   11   12

Chapter Four: Basic Improvisation

Pentatonic Scales

Pentatonic scales are actually the basis for the blues scale. They are five-note scales (*penta* is the Greek word for "five"). If you take the $^\flat$5 out of the blues scale, you get a minor pentatonic scale.

The G Blues Scale	G – B$^\flat$ – C – D$^\flat$– D – F 1 – $^\flat$3 – 4 – $^\flat$5 – 5 –$^\flat$7
The G Minor Pentatonic Scale	G – B$^\flat$ – C – D – F 1 – $^\flat$3 – 4 – 5 – $^\flat$7

Either one of these scales will work over a blues progression in G. Here is something very cool to know: so will an E Blues scale! The following diagram will show you why:

The E Blues Scale	E – G – A – B – B – D
Numbered in E	1 – $^\flat$3 – 4 –$^\flat$5 – 5 – $^\flat$7
Numbered in G	6 – 1 – 2 –$^\flat$3– 3 – $^\flat$5

The E Blues scale has a lot in common with the G Blues scale—the 1, $^\flat$3 and$^\flat$5. Plus, the B, which is 3 in G, works great over a G7 chord. This will work with any blues scale. Just think down three letters in the alphabet and you will find a very closely related blues scale. Try A and C, or F and D, etc.

G Blues Scale

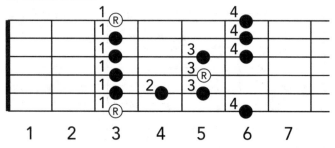

E Blues Scale

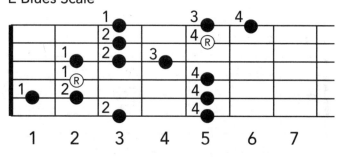

Blues Guitar for Adults

Now here's another interesting thing. Look at the E Blues scale. Make G the root, remove the B♭ and you get the G Major Pentatonic scale!

This will also sound great over a blues in G (but not a minor blues in G!).

The G Major Pentatonic Scale	G – A – B*– D – E
	1 – 2 – 3*– 5 – 6

*No ♭3! That's why it's *major*!

The moral of the story is that although there's lots of confusion out there about the blues scale and the pentatonic scales, they are all pretty much the same things. The distinctions are theoretically subtle. It's all in how you use them and the context you use them in.

USING THE MAJOR PENTATONIC SCALE OVER IV7 AND V7

A colorful way to play over the IV7 chord (C7 in G) and the V chord (D7 in G) is to use each chord's major pentatonic scale. Notice that in the diagrams below, we have kept both scales around the third position. It is helpful to learn to stay in the same area of the neck as you change from one scale to another. Your playing will sound much smoother and more natural this way. Avoid the temptation to simply move the same scale pattern to a different root. Use a different pattern and stay in the same general area.

C MAJOR PENTATONIC SCALE

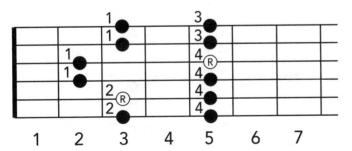

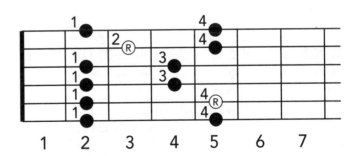

The following licks are examples of mixing the minor and major pentatonic scales over the I chord, G7. You will find the G Blues scale (minor pentatonic) and the E Blues scale (G Major Pentatonic). Most good blues players are continually combining scales in this way to create strong blues licks.

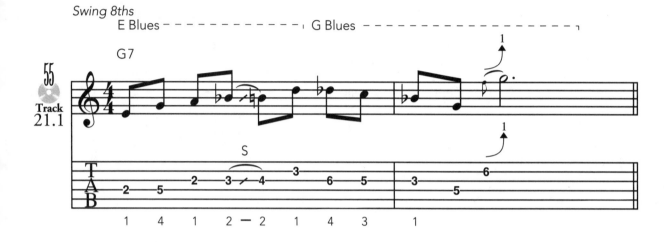

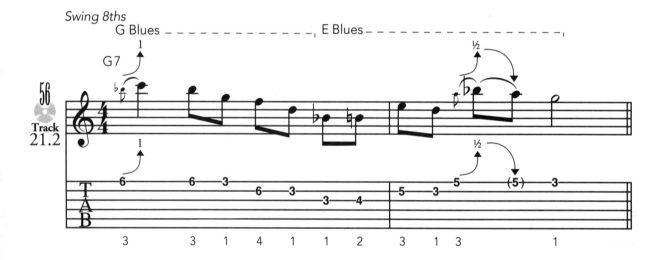

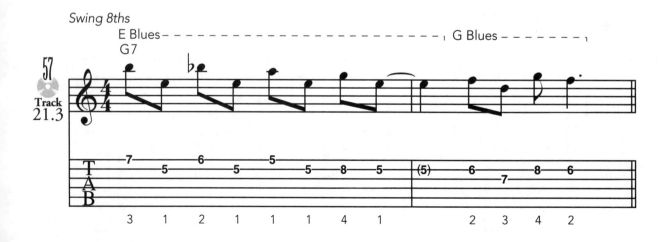

Blues Guitar for Adults

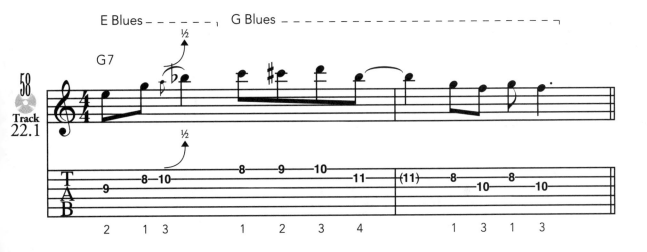

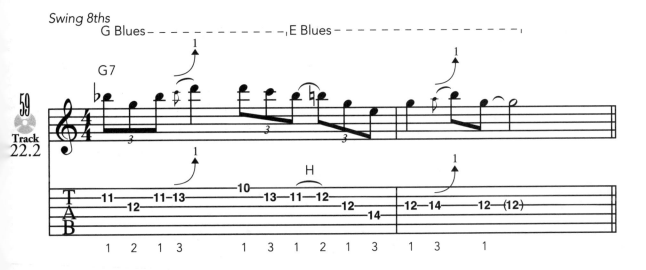

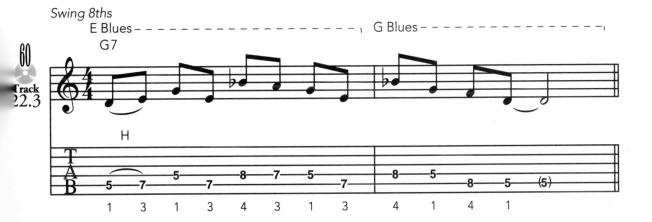

Chapter Four: Basic Improvisation

The following licks are derived from the A Blues scale (C Major Pentatonic) patterns. In G, you can use this scale over the IV chord, C7.

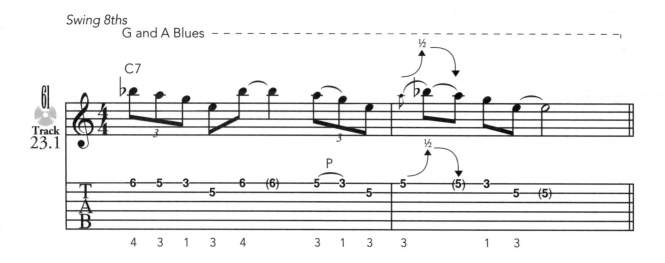

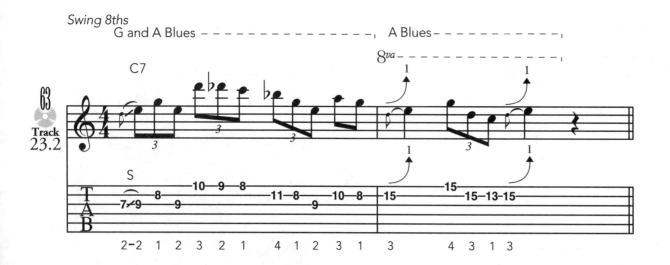

Blues Guitar for Adults

These last two examples are derived from
the B Blues scale (D Major Pentatonic).
This scale works for licks over the V chord,
D7, in the key of G.

*"I wanted to learn more about blues technique
and become a better player. I enjoy learning music theory
and understanding improvisational ideas."*

Monique Turner, 39
Administrative Assistant

Chapter Four: Basic Improvisation

Chapter Five
minor blues

In the most common minor blues progressions, the I–IV–V chord structure remains intact except that minor 7 chords are used instead of dominant 7 chords. On the right are the i7, iv7 and v7 chords (remember, for minor chords we use lower case Roman numerals) in two important minor keys.

Key	i7	iv7	v7
E Minor	Emin7	Amin7	Bmin7
A Minor	Amin7	Dmin7	Emin7

Play this example in E Minor as shown. Then, using the chart above, transpose it to the key of A Minor.

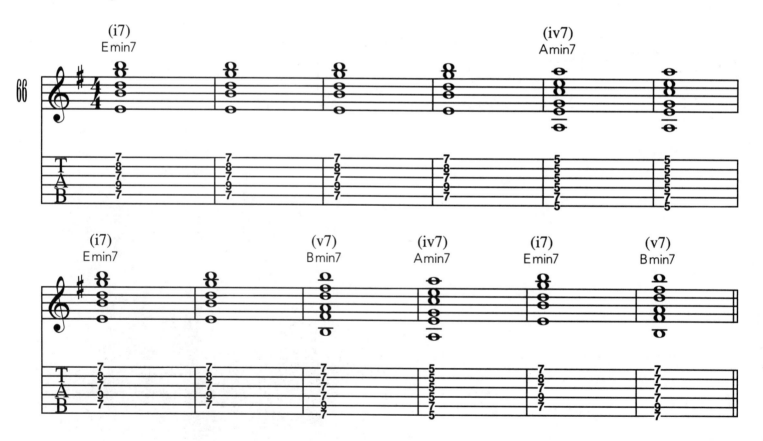

In this next A Minor example, watch for the quick change to the iv7 chord, Dmin7, in bar 2. Also notice the VI–V7–i–V7 progression in the last four bars (see page 22). This is in the style of B.B. King's "The Thrill Is Gone."

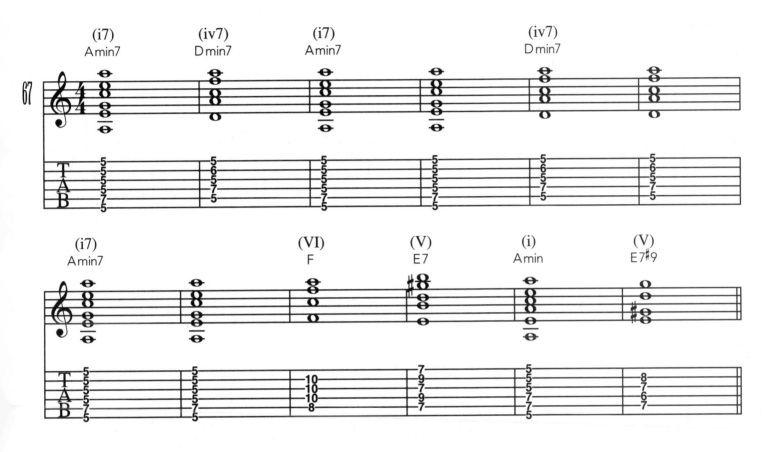

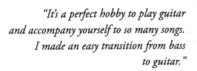

"It's a perfect hobby to play guitar and accompany yourself to so many songs. I made an easy transition from bass to guitar."

Chapter Five: Minor Blues

Natural Minor Scales

Now let's learn the five patterns for the A and E Natural Minor scales. The natural minor scale (1–2–♭3–4–5–♭6–♭7–8) is often combined with the blues scale to create licks over minor blues progressions.

A NATURAL MINOR

Pattern #1
Pattern #2

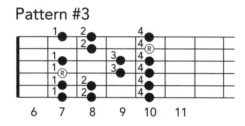
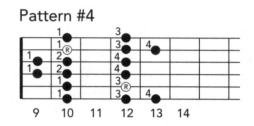

Pattern #3
Pattern #4

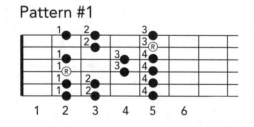
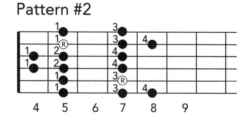

Pattern #5

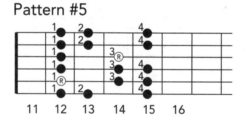

E NATURAL MINOR

Pattern #1
Pattern #2

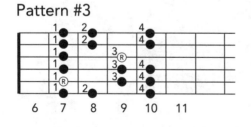
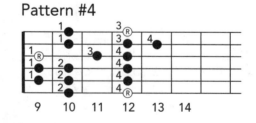

Pattern #3
Pattern #4

Pattern #5

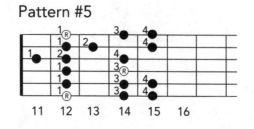

Blues Guitar for Adults

Now let's look at combining the natural minor scale with the blues scale. In this case, the scale you use should always have the same root as the key you are playing in. For example, to play over an A Minor progression, use the A Blues scale (A–C–D–E♭–E–G) and the A Minor scale (A–B–C–D–E–F–G–A); to play over the key of E Minor, use the E Blues scale (E–G–A–B♭–B–D) and the E Natural Minor scale (E–F♯–G–A–B–C–D–E); and so on.

Here are some examples of how these scales can be used together.

Chapter Six
arpeggios

The next phase of blues improvising involves *arpeggios*. An arpeggio is a broken chord or the individual notes of a chord played separately. Instead of playing a scale, you just play the tones of the chord you are jamming over.

 Dominant 7 Arpeggios

Let's start with the dominant 7 arpeggios in an A blues (A7, D7 and E7). As with the major pentatonic scales on page 37, all three arpeggios are presented in the same area of the neck—between the 3rd and 7th frets. This is so you can practice staying in the same area as you change harmonies. The same concept as described on page 37 is at work here— your playing will sound smoother and more natural this way. Avoid simply moving the same finger pattern around to different locations on the neck.

I7: The A7 Arpeggio   A – C♯ – E – G
                           1 – 3 – 5 – ♭7

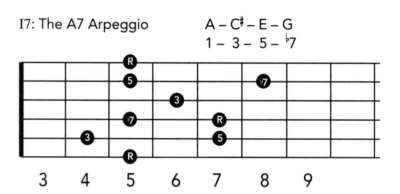

IV7: The D7 Arpeggio   D – F♯ – A – C
                           1 – 3 – 5 – ♭7

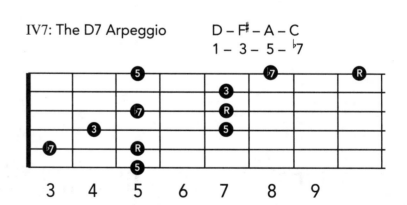

Practice playing over a twelve-bar blues in A, playing the appropriate arpeggio over each chord in the progression.

V7: The E7 Arpeggio   E – G# – B– D
                       1 – 3 – 5 –♭7

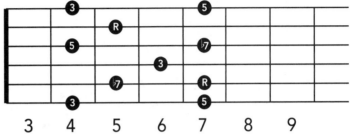

Now let's repeat the same process between the 9th and 12th frets. When you have the arpeggios mastered, try playing them over a blues in A, switching arpeggios as the chords change.

I7: The A7 Arpeggio   A – C# – E – G
                       1 – 3 – 5 – ♭7

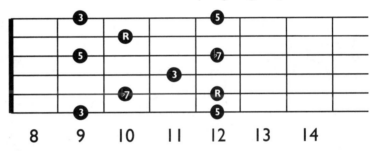

IV7: The D7 Arpeggio   D – F# – A – C
                        1 – 3 – 5 – ♭7

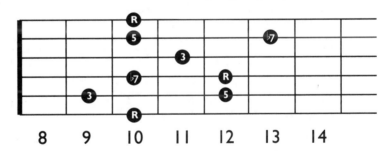

V7: The E7 Arpeggio   E – G# – B – D
                       1 – 3 – 5 – ♭7

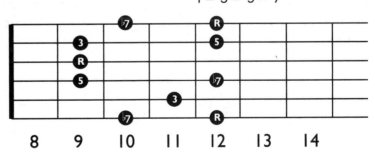

Chapter Six: Arpeggios

The following examples use combinations of dominant 7 arpeggios and the blues scale. By mixing scale and arpeggio licks together, you can create powerful improvisational ideas over blues progressions. We will stay in the key of A, and work on some licks for the chord (A7).

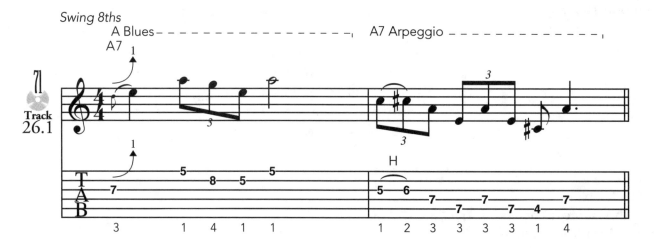

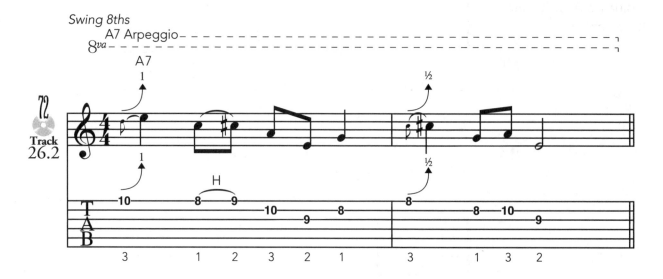

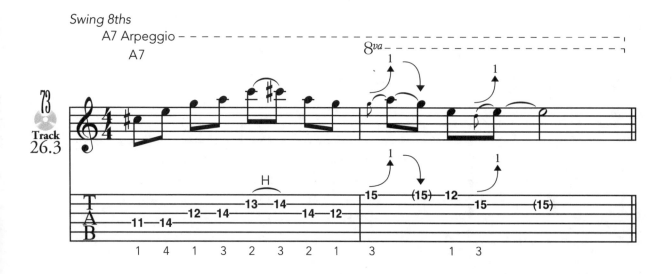

Blues Guitar for Adults

Let's continue in the key of A and build licks over the IV7 (D7) and V7 (E7) chords using the arpeggios of each chord combined with the blues scales.

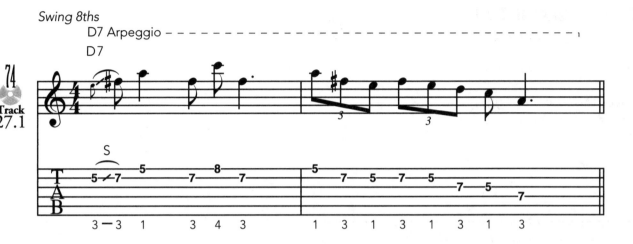

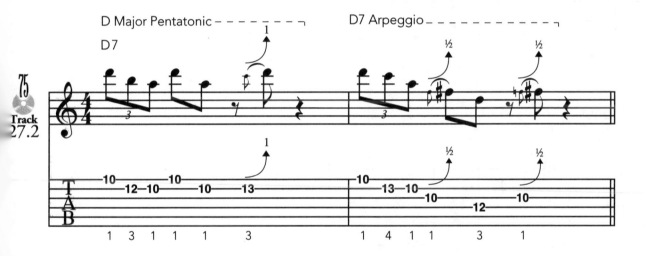

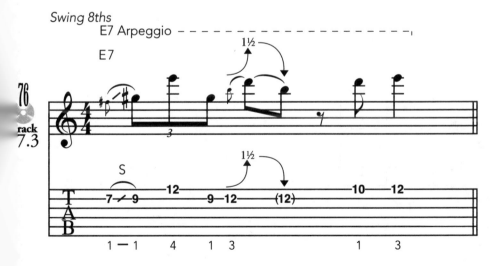

Minor 7 Arpeggios

Let's learn the arpeggios for the minor 7 chords. Memorize each arpeggio over the i7–iv7–v7 A Minor blues progression. Once again, notice how each arpeggio stays in the same area of the neck.

i7: The Amin7 Arpeggio   A – C – E – G
                           1 – $\flat$3 – 5 – $\flat$7

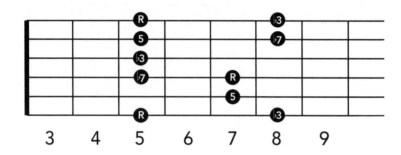

iv7: The Dmin7 Arpeggio   D – F – A – C
                            1 – $\flat$3 – 5 – $\flat$7

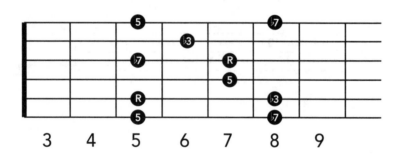

v7: The Emin7 Arpeggio   E – G – B – D
                           1 – $\flat$3 – 5 – $\flat$7

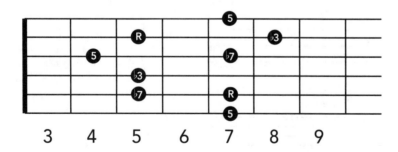

Let's do the same routine between the 9th and 12th frets. Practice using these arpeggios over an A Minor blues.

i7: The Amin7 Arpeggio   A – C – E – G
                           1 – ♭3 – 5 – 7

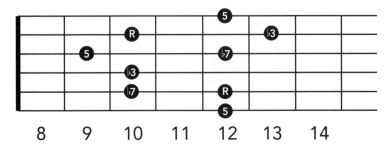

iv7: The Dmin7 Arpeggio   D – F – A – C
                            1 – ♭3 – 5 – ♭7

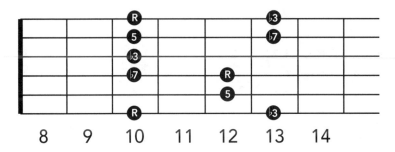

v7: The Emin7 Arpeggio   E – G – B – D
                           1 – ♭3 – 5 – ♭7

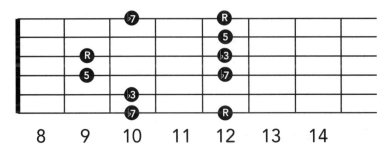

Chapter Six: Arpeggios

The following examples use combinations of minor 7 arpeggios, the blues scale and natural minor scale. This "composite thinking" establishes strong musical lines over a minor blues tune. Let's start with licks over the i7 chord in A Minor, Amin7.

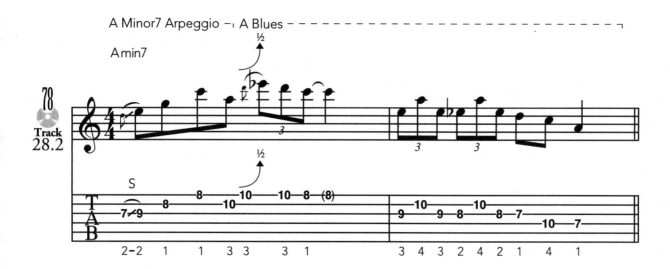

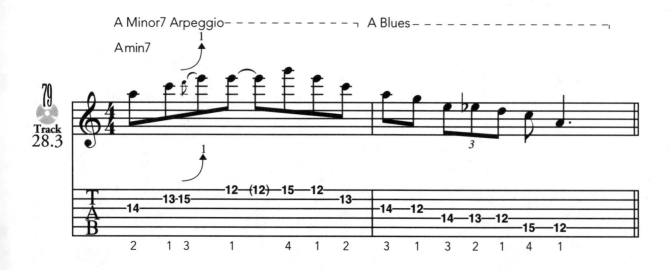

Blues Guitar for Adults

Staying in A Minor, let's continue with licks over the iv7 (Dmin7) and v7 (Emin7) chords using the arpeggios of each chord combined with the blues scale or natural minor scale.

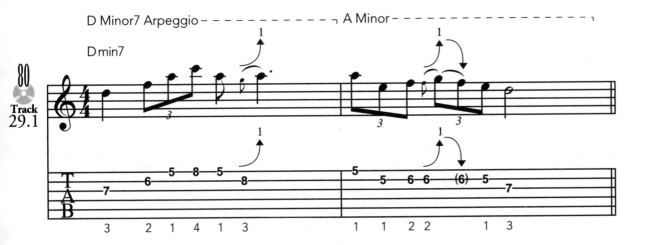

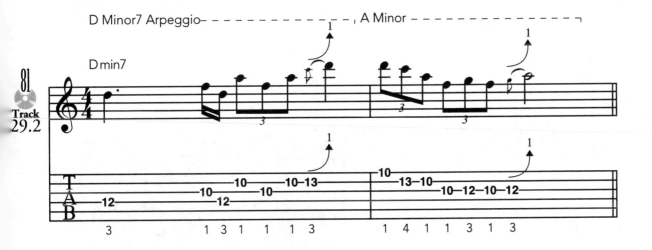

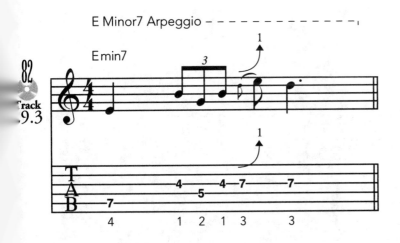

Chapter Six: Arpeggios

Chapter Seven
improvising over I7–IV7–V7 in E

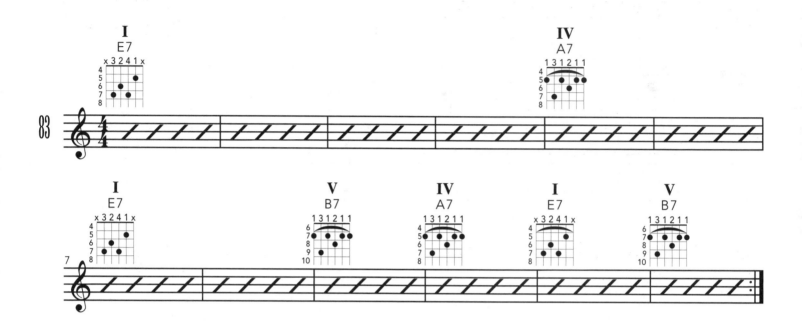

Study the Texas-style style solo on the following page (page 55). It should be played at a medium fast tempo. The notes over the I chord lean heavily towards the E Minor Pentatonic scale. Arpeggios over the IV and V chords are common in this style.

Let's look at the style of Freddie King. He was the most influential Texas rocker in blues history. He was the major force in shaping the styles of Eric Clapton, Stevie Ray Vaughan and many others. His pop chart hit, "Hideaway," established him as an important player during the 1960s and '70s. His recording of "The Key to the Highway" is a classic. King's string bending, vibrato and double-stop techniques (where lines are played in intervals such as a 3rd) were impeccable. Learn the six licks in the style of King and apply them to a twelve-bar blues.

Freddie King

Freddie King was the major force in shaping the styles of Eric Clapton, Stevie Ray Vaughan and many others. His pop chart hit, "Hideaway," established him as an important player during the 1960s and '70s.

PHOTO • CHUCK PULIN/COURTESY OF STAR FILE, INC.

55

Twelve-Bar Blues Solo in E

Chapter Seven: Improvising Over I7–IV7–V7 in E

Licks in the Style of Freddie King

Learn the following six licks in the style of Freddie King and apply them to a twelve-bar blues.

A repetitive triplet figure is always a strong motif for an opening blues lick. The descending blues scale across adjacent patterns is a refreshing change from always running licks in the same pattern. This one moves from Pattern #4 to Pattern #3.

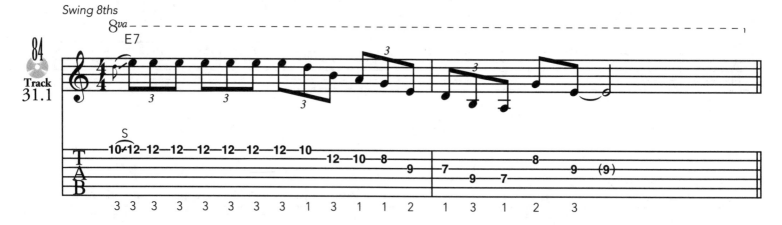

Here's a slick example of the E Minor Pentatonic and E Major Pentatonic scales mixing in the same area of the neck to create a colorful lick.

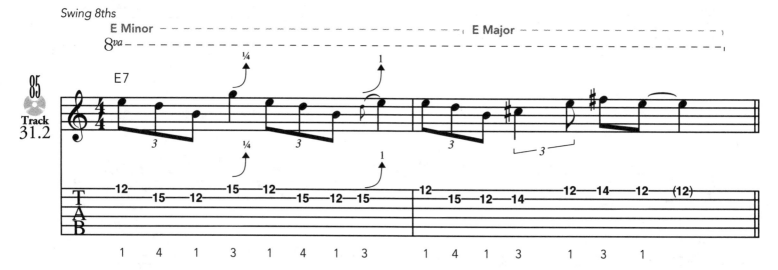

This is a classic Delta blues "train-whistle" lick followed by a lick in the E Mixolydian mode. The Mixolydian mode is a major scale with a lowered 7th degree (1–2–3–4–5–6–♭7). See page 94 for a look at Mixolydian fingering.

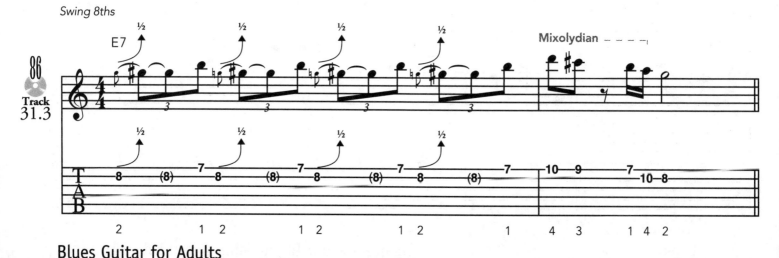

Blues Guitar for Adults

This is a IV chord lick that accents the notes of the A7 chord. The addition of the note B on the 7th fret of the high E string adds the colorful 9th tone.

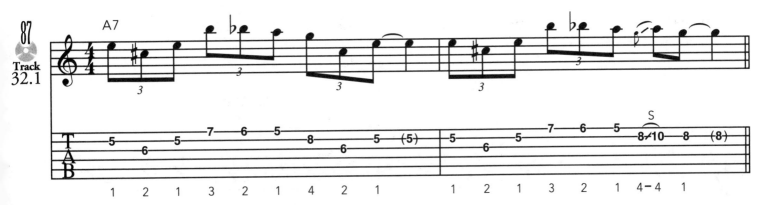

This **IV** chord lick hangs in the main E Minor Pentatonic scale box (transpose the fingering on page 36) but accents the notes of the A7 chord.

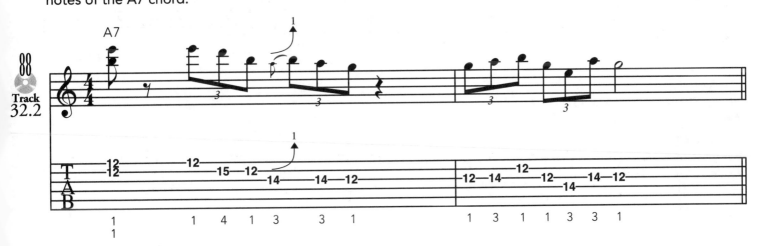

This IV chord lick uses harmonized major and minor 3rd intervals in the B Mixolydian mode (see page 94). It is definitely in the style of Freddie King.

Chapter Seven: Improvising Over I7–IV7–V7 in E

Chapter Eight
improvising over I7–IV7–V7 in A

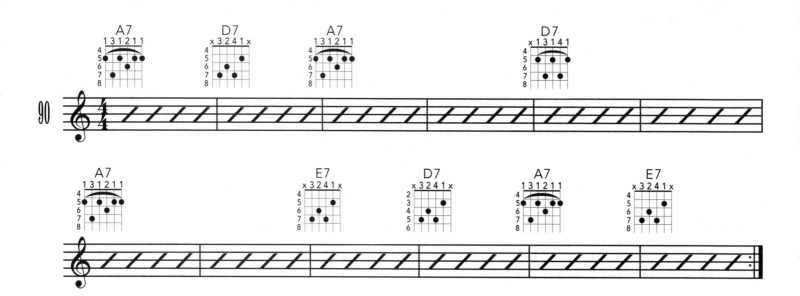

Study the slow blues solo on page 58. An even mixture of the A Major and Minor Pentatonic scales is very effective over a slow blues. For IV7 and V7, use each chord's major pentatonic scale. Over IV7 (D7), use D Major Pentatonic and over V7 (E7), use E Major Pentatonic. Notice the numerous bends over a slower blues tempo.

In this chapter, we'll investigate the style of Mike Bloomfield. He was the most soulful blues player ever. His work with the Paul Butterfield Blues Band brought him much attention as an improviser who played all the right notes with soulful bends and fluid phrasing. His playing on the "Super Session" album with keyboardist Al Kooper and the first Electric Flag album, "A Long Time Comin'," is flawless. His untimely death in the late 1970s was a terrible loss to the blues community.

Twelve-Bar Blues Solo in A

Chapter Eight: Improvising Over I7–IV7–V7 in A

Licks in the Style of Mike Bloomfield

Learn the following six licks in the style of Mike Bloomfield and apply them to a twelve-bar blues.

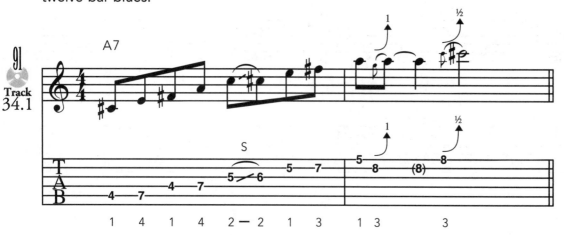

This straight-ahead A Minor Pentatonic lick is highlighted by the addition of the major 3rd, C#, in bar 1. The blending of the A Major Pentatonic scale (in bar 1) and the A Minor Pentatonic scale (in bar 2) is always sweet.

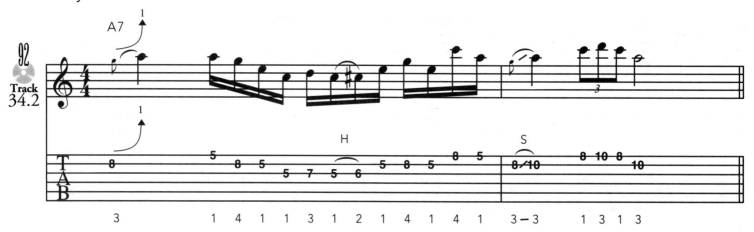

Here's another example of how Bloomfield might have used the powerful combination of the major and minor 3rd tones in the same lick. The C# note is the major 3rd of the A Major Pentatonic scale, and the C note is the minor 3rd of the A Minor Pentatonic scale.

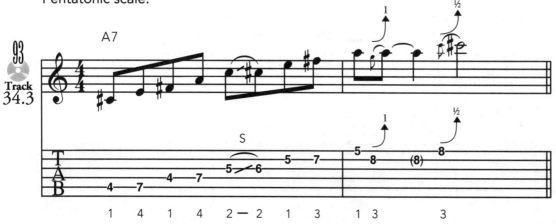

Blues Guitar for Adults

Here's a IV-chord lick staying in the A Blues scale, but accenting the notes of the D7 chord.

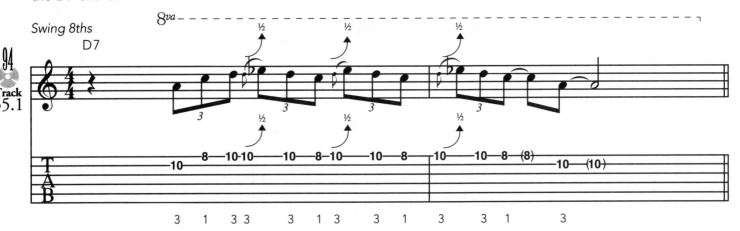

This one is a IV-chord lick derived from the D Major Pentatonic scale but ending with the bluesy ♭7-to-root bend. The major pentatonic scale is always a strong choice over the IV chord.

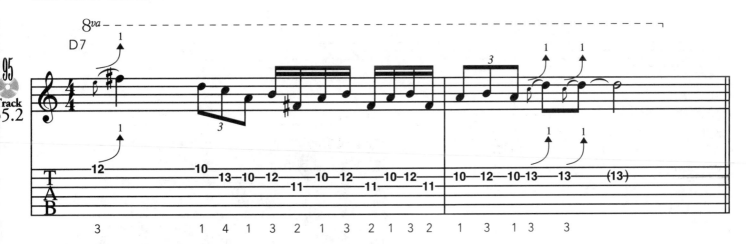

This V-chord lick starts out with the E Mixolydian mode (see page 94 for a transposable fingering) and ends by using both the major and minor 3rd. The major 3rd note, G♯, fits in the E7 chord.

The minor 3rd note, G♮, is a bit harsher but works because the ♭3rd is another way of spelling a ♯9. This is a colorful chord extension that our ears accept as normal.

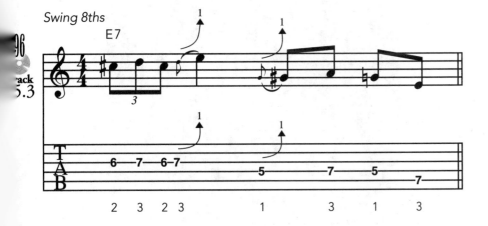

Chapter Eight: Improvising Over I7–IV7–V7 in A

Chapter Nine
improvising over I7–IV7–V7 in G

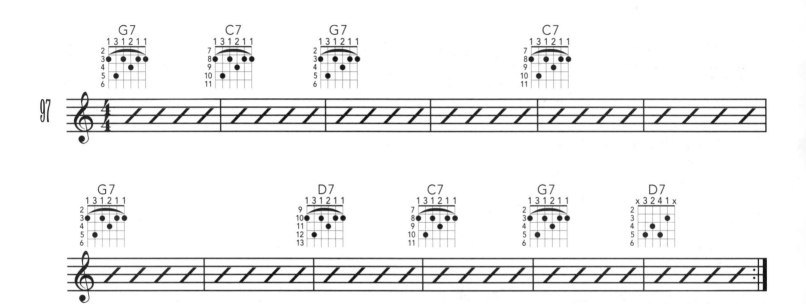

Study the medium-tempo rock-blues solo on page 63. Notice the mix of straight-eighth and triplet rhythms. Rely mainly on the minor pentatonic scale over the I chord and chord tones over the IV and V chords.

In this chapter, we'll take a look at the style of Eric Clapton. Clapton became well known from his work with the Yardbirds, Cream and John Mayall's Blues Breakers. He has always had universal appeal to rock and blues afficionados alike. His work on the first Mayall album brought instant recognition to the Chicago blues sound and validated it to a wide range of the rock audience in the mid 1960s. He has continued to carry the blues banner with *Clapton Unplugged* and *Back to the Cradle*.

Eric Clapton

Eric Clapton's work on the first Mayall album brought instant recognition to the Chicago blues sound and validated it to a wide range of the rock audience in the mid 1960s.

PHOTO • BOB GRUEN/COURTESY OF STAR FILE, INC.

Twelve-Bar Blues Solo in G

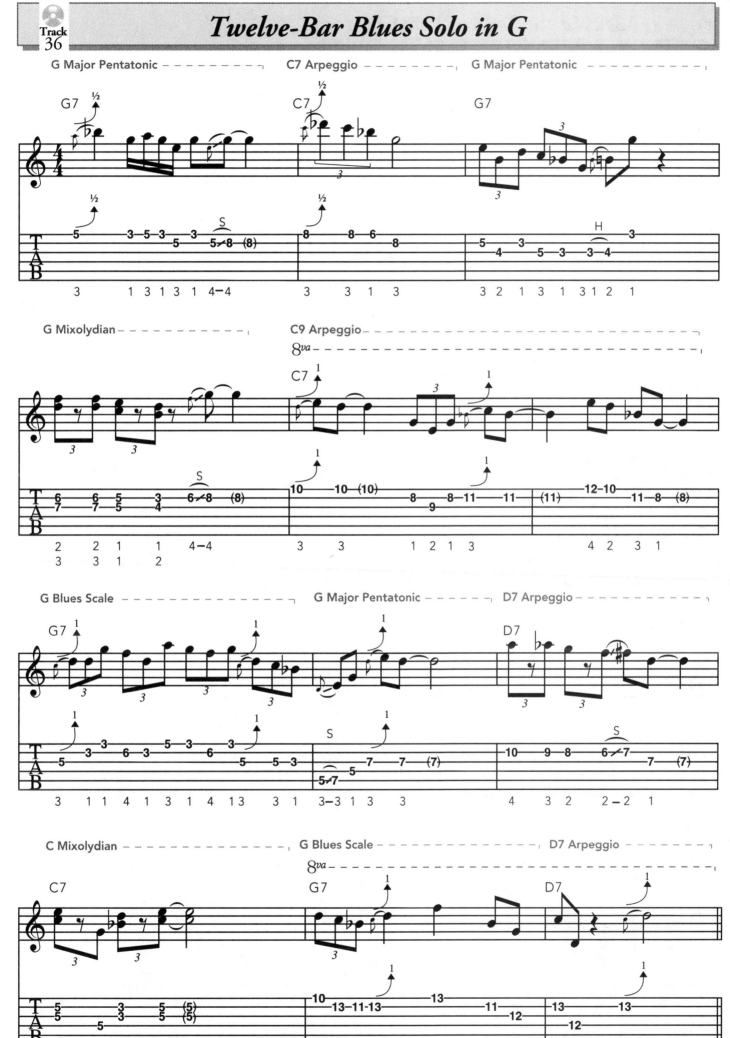

Chapter Nine: Improvising Over I7–IV7–V7 in G

Licks in the Style of Eric Clapton

Learn the following six licks in the style of Eric Clapton and apply them to a twelve-bar blues.

Here's a typical G Minor Pentatonic scale lick in the style of Clapton. Bend the last note down and choke it.

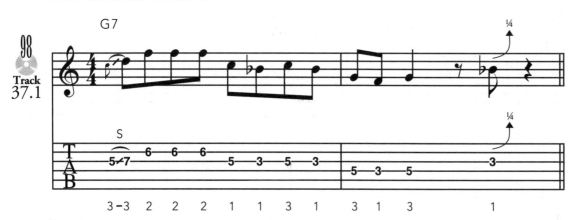

It's the contour of this G Minor Pentatonic lick that makes it work. The notes ascend, descend, ascend back and them descend to the root note, G.

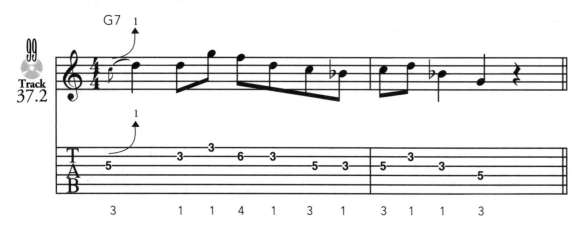

Here's an E Blues scale lick highlighted by the bend-release-pull-off technique in bar 2. The E Blues scale is the same scale as the G Major Pentatonic scale with an added B♭ note.

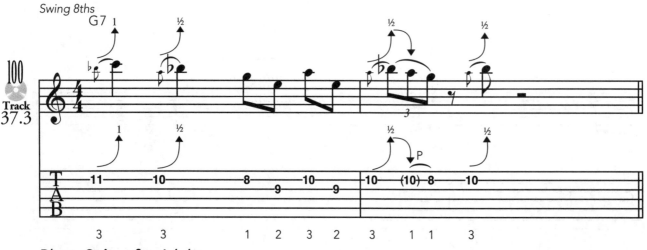

Blues Guitar for Adults

This IV-chord lick stays in the main G Minor Pentatonic scale box but accents the notes of the C7 chord.

This IV-chord lick uses a classic repetitive blues phrase followed by a colorful C Mixolydian lick.

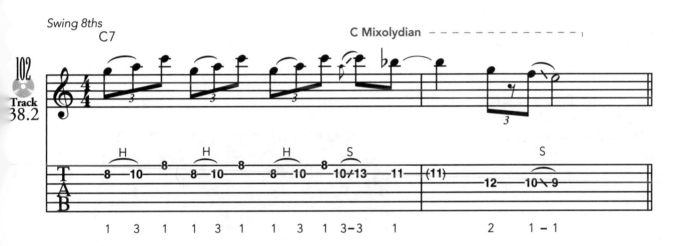

This V-chord lick approaches the root of the V chord, D7, by normal freting, sliding and bending. In the blues, it's less what you play than the way you play it!

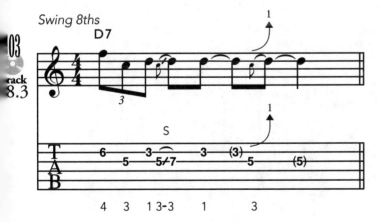

Chapter Nine: Improvising Over I7–IV7–V7 in G

Chapter Ten
improvising over I7–IV7–V7 in C

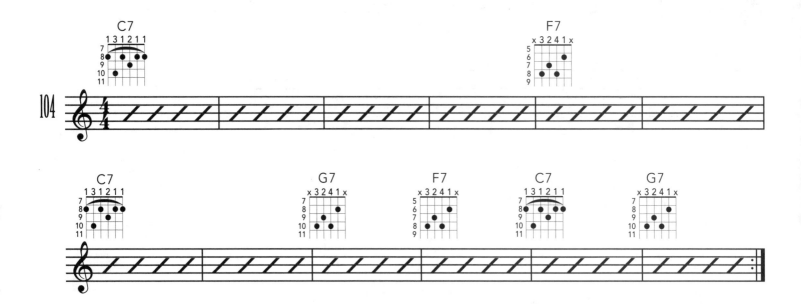

Study the medium-slow Chicago blues style solo on page 67. The whole solo is played in the C Minor Pentatonic scale in the eighth position. The slides, hammers and bends keep the solo bluesy.

In this chapter, we'll study the style of Muddy Waters. He brought the Mississippi Delta-blues sound to Chicago in 1943. He established the "uptown" or Chicago blues sound by using the electric guitar to play over the din of the blues clubs. He single-handedly transformed the rural folk idiom of delta blues to an urban popular music. His haunting licks and biting slide guitar work became the trademark for all electric blues players to come.

Muddy Waters

Muddy Waters brought the Mississippi Delta-blues sound to Chicago in 1943.

Twelve-Bar Blues Solo in C

Chapter Ten: Improvising Over I7–IV7–V7 in C

Licks in the Style of Muddy Waters

Learn the six licks in the style of Muddy Waters and apply them a twelve-bar blues.

This classic C Minor Pentatonic lick slides between adjacent blues scale patterns (#5 and #1, see page 34).

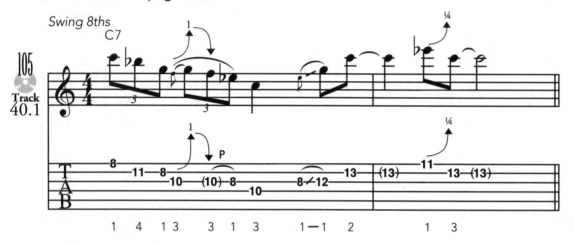

A double-string blues lick in the style of Muddy Waters revolving around notes of the C Mixolydian mode (see page 94) accenting the notes of a C Major triad.

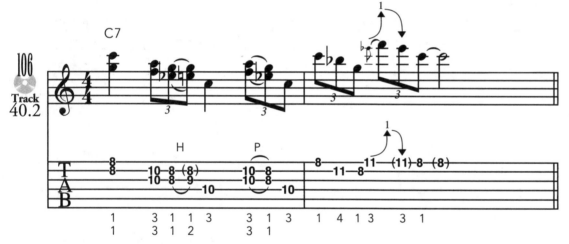

A C Minor Pentatonic scale lick on the lower strings reminiscent of the Delta blues sound.

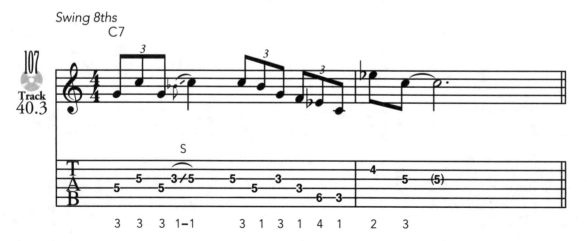

Blues Guitar for Adults

Here's a IV chord Delta blues-based lick featuring a wailing F7 chord triplet figure followed by a C Minor idea.

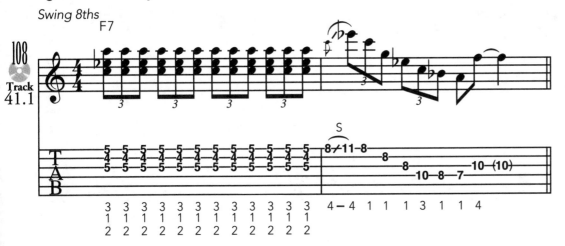

This IV-chord lick uses soulful bends on the high E string from the C Minor Pentatonic scale, although the tones of the F7 chord are highlighted.

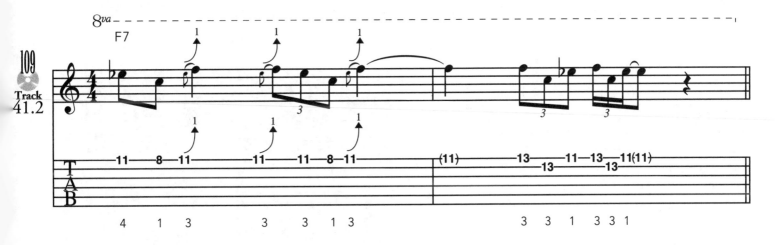

This V-chord lick arpeggiates the G7 chord.

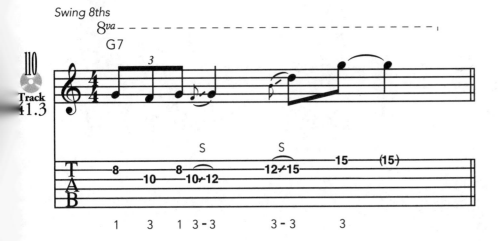

Chapter Ten: Improvising Over I7–IV7–V7 in C

Chapter Eleven
improvising over i7–iv7–v7 in A Minor

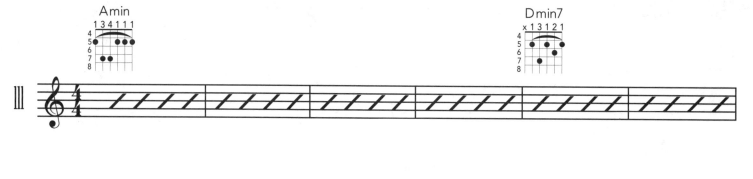

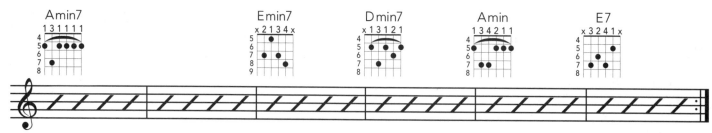

Study the medium tempo minor blues solo on page 71. The A Blues scale is the primary source for soloing over the i7 chord. The A Minor scale works effectively over the iv7 and v7 chords, particularly if you highlight the chord tones of each.

This chapter investigates the style of Albert King. He played left-handed with the strings upside down but in order. Hailing from the same town as B. B. King—Indianola, Mississippi—he moved to Memphis where blues was thriving in the early 1960s. His appearances at the Fillmore Theatres helped launch his popularity with rock audiences. He was a dynamic performer who played with an economy of notes and excellent string bending technique. His *Live Wire/Blues Power* remains a classic recording.

PHOTO • BARRIE WENTZELL/COURTESY OF STAR FILE, INC.

Albert King moved to Memphis where blues was thriving in the early 1960s. His Live Wire/Blues Power *remains a classic recording.*

A Twelve-Bar Blues Solo in A Minor

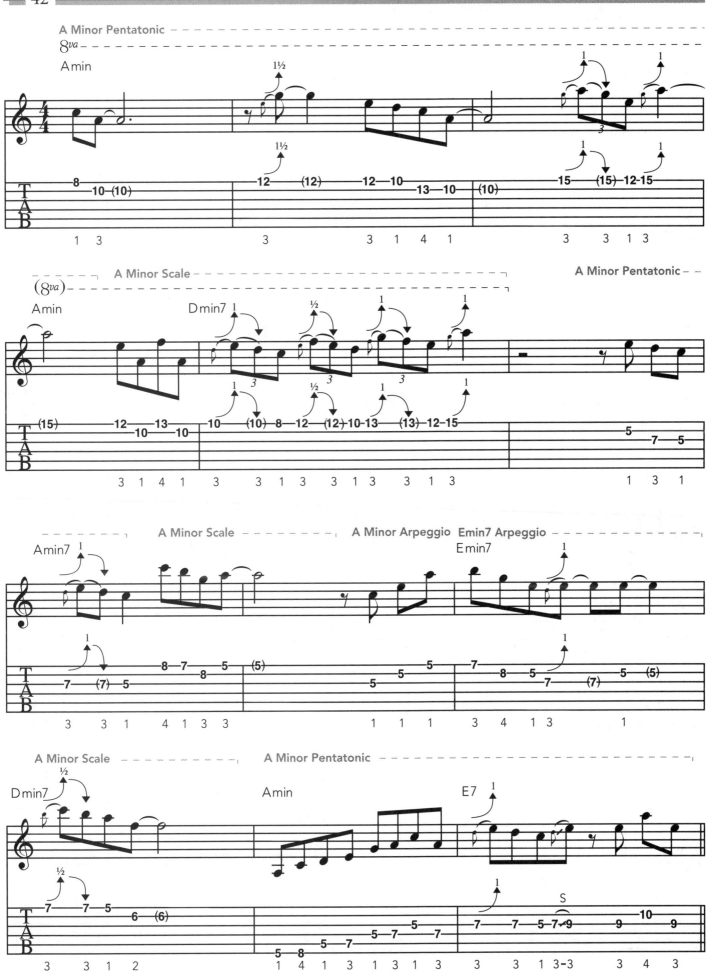

Chapter Eleven: Improvising Over i7–iv7–v7 in A Minor

Licks in the Style of Albert King

Here are some licks in the style of Albert King.

The A Minor Pentatonic scale works well over the i7 chord because the notes of the chord (Amin7), A, C, E and G, are all contained in the scale.

The sixteenth-note pattern in this lick is made up of notes from the A Minor Pentatonic scale. The second bar ends this balanced lick with a simpler A Minor arpeggio.

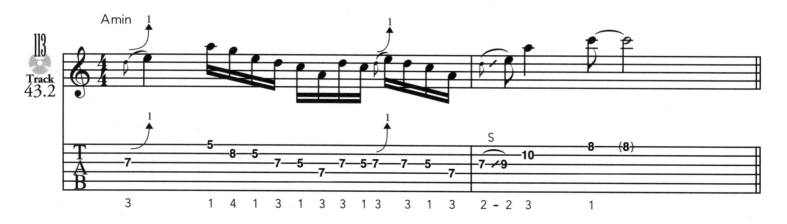

This A Minor Pentatonic lick is highlighted by the opening minor-3rd bends from the 5th to the ♭7th.

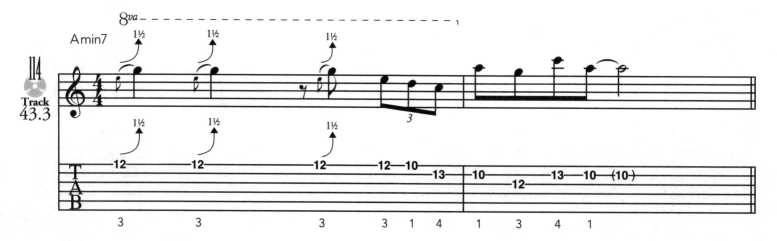

Blues Guitar for Adults

This iv-chord lick slips into the E Minor scale but features the notes of the Dmin7 chord. When playing over iv7 and v7 in a minor blues, you can use the minor scale built on the root of each chord.

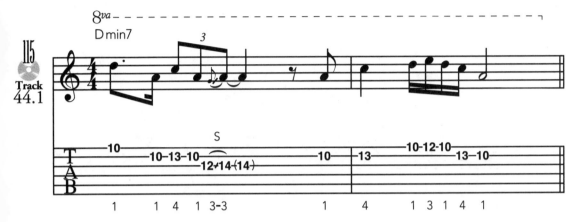

Here's a gutsy iv-chord lick in the style of Albert King that uses the A Minor Pentatonic scale but highlights the notes of the Dmin7 chord.

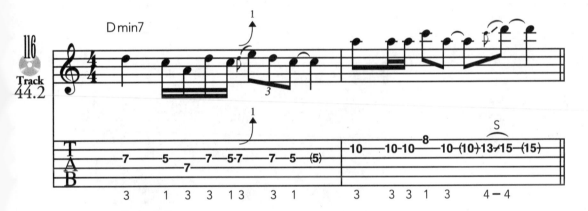

This v-chord lick revolves from the ♭7th (D) to the root note (E) and back.

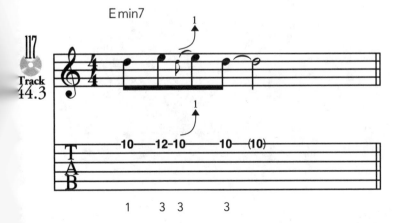

Chapter Eleven: Improvising Over i7–iv7–v7 in A Minor

Chapter Twelve
improvising over i7–iv7–v7 in E Minor

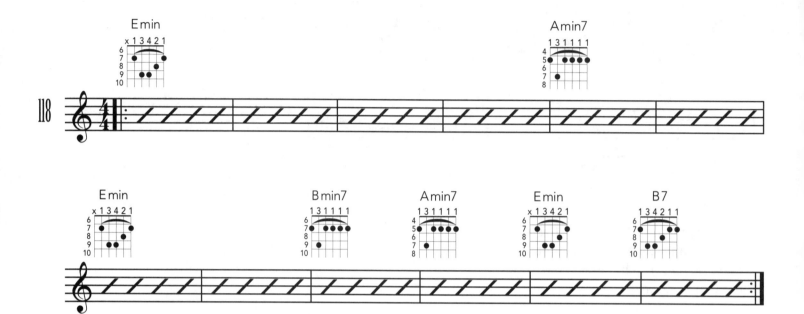

Study the slow minor blues solo on page 75. Notice the philosophy of "less is more" throughout. Make the bends sing with strong vibrato. The mixture of the E Minor scale with the E Minor Pentatonic scale gives this minor blues solo color and depth.

In this chapter, we'll look at the style of Robert Cray. He helped to revitalize the popularity of the blues with rock-crazed audiences in the 1980s. Born in Georgia but a military brat most of his childhood, his 1986 *Strong Persuader* album had a pop feel that captured a wide audience. He sings classic blues lyrics that everyone can relate to. His greatest strengths are his smooth style and excellent tone.

Robert Cray helped to regain the popularity of the blues with rock-crazed audiences in the 1980s.

PHOTO • GENE SHAW/COURTESY OF STAR FILE, INC.

Twelve-Bar Blues Solo in E Minor

Chapter Twelve: Improvising Over i7–iv7–v7 in E Minor

Licks in the Style of Robert Cray

Learn the following six licks in the style of Robert Cray and apply them to a twelve-bar blues.

This E Minor Pentatonic scale lick is highlighted by the minor-3rd bend from E to G.

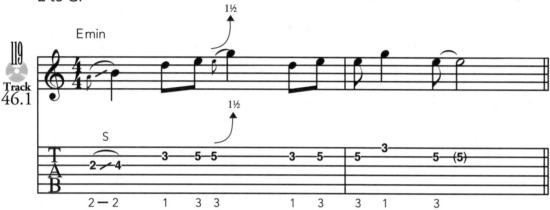

Here's a straight-ahead E Minor Pentatonic scale lick with standard bends.

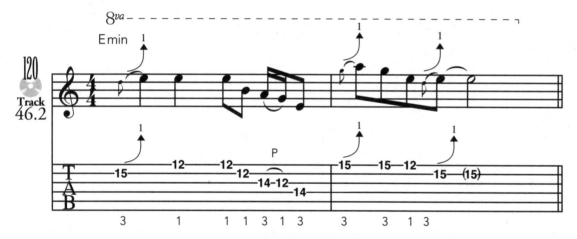

This classic double-string figure out of the E blues scale is definitely in the style of Cray. Make sure the E on the 12th fret on the high E string rings strongly.

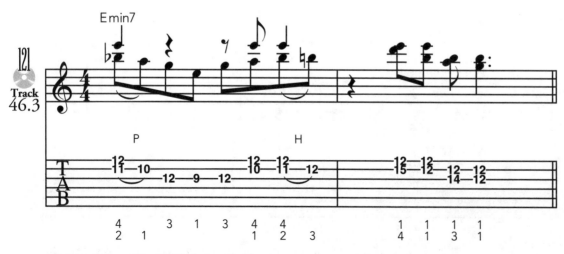

Blues Guitar for Adults

Here's a iv-chord lick starting with an Amin7 arpeggio and ending with notes out of the E Minor scale highlighting the Amin7 chord.

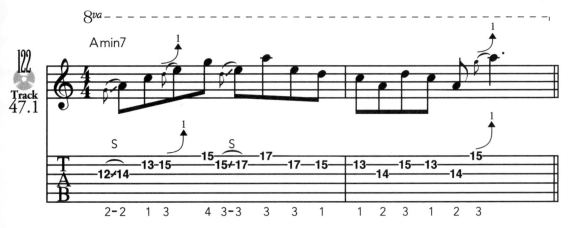

This classic iv-chord lick opens with a repetitive A Minor arpeggio figure in bar 1 and closes with notes from the A Blues scale.

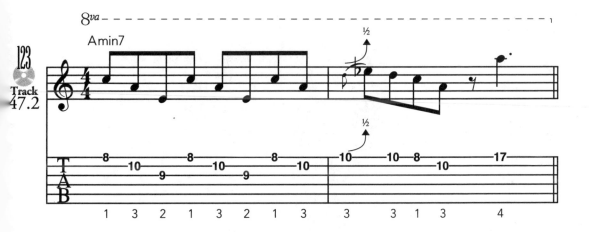

This is a v-chord lick out of the E Minor scale highlighting the notes of the Bmin7 chord.

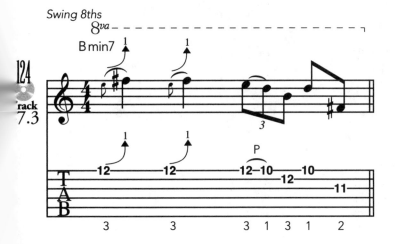

Chapter Twelve: Improvising Over i7–iv7–v7 in E Minor

Chapter Thirteen
improvising over gospel blues changes in D

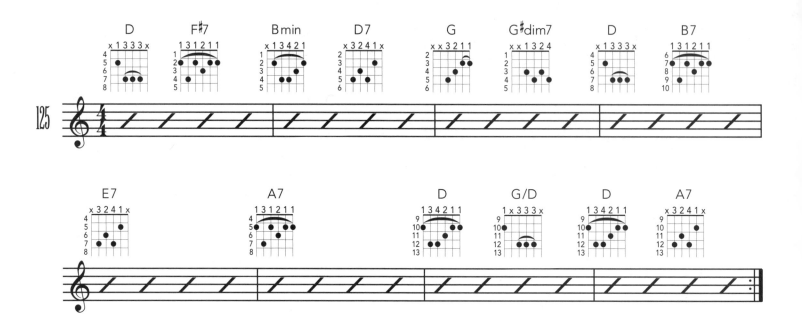

Study the medium-slow gospel blues solo on page 79. This is a tricky form to improvise over because there are lots of chords that change more rapidly than in a standard blues. The D Major Pentatonic scale is the main source for the notes in this solo over the short, eight-bar form. In bars 3 through 6, you need to play specific chord tones over each chord. Double-string licks should be interjected as much as possible.

Let's take a look at the style of B. B. King. The greatest blues man of them all, he has averaged three hundred gigs a year over the past forty years. His pioneering technique of raking and sweeping the strings, along with his vicious wrist vibrato, has made him the most emulated blues player ever. His economical use of notes and ability to play tastefully over many blues styles with just the right touch has kept him at the throne as King of the Blues. His *Live at the Regal* recording in 1964 is astounding. A decade later, "The Thrill Is Gone" propelled him to household name satus.

B. B. King

PHOTO • AL PEREIRA/COURTESY OF STAR FILE, INC.

B. B. King has averaged three hundred gigs a year over the past forty years. His Live at the Regal *recording in 1964 is astounding.*

Eight-Bar Blues Solo in D

Chapter Thirteen: Improvising Over Gospel Blues Changes in D

Licks in the Style of B. B. King

Learn the following six licks in the style of B. B. King and apply them to the eight-bar form.

In this lick, the D Major Pentatonic scale works very well over I (D) and III7 (F♯7).

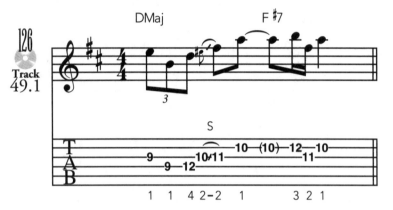

Here's a soulful, repetitive, string-bend lick built on the D Major Pentatonic scale.

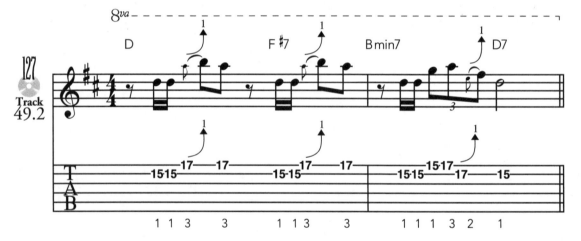

This is a G Major arpeggio lick over the IV chord (G) followed by a G♯ Diminished scale (see page 94) lick over the G♯ dim7 chord.

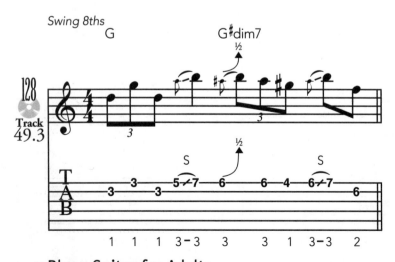

Blues Guitar for Adults

Here we have the D Major Pentatonic scale followed by a B7 arpeggio. Notice the bend on the last note into the 5th (F#).

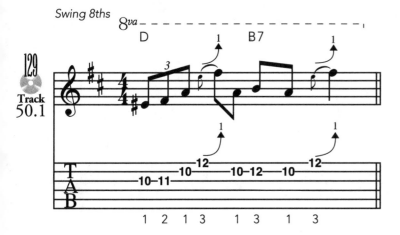

This is a classic lick with passing tones. Passing tones, in this case D#, are notes that don't belong to the harmony and are used to connect chord tones. This lick uses the E Mixolydian mode (see page 94) over the E7 chord, followed by the A Mixolydian mode over the A7 chord.

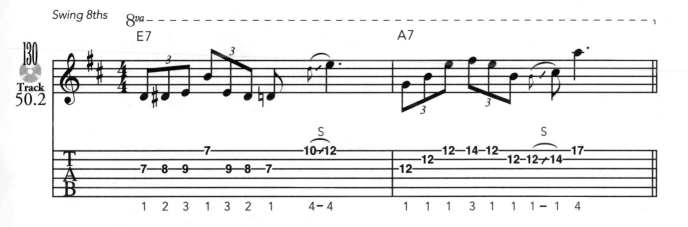

This standard turnaround lick uses consecutive major arpeggios over the D and G chords.

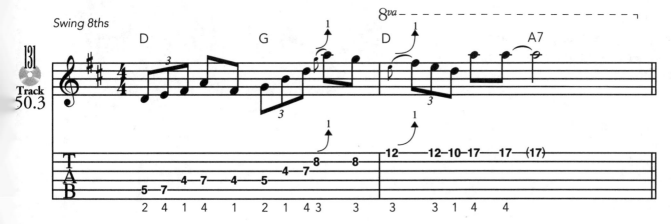

Chapter Thirteen: Improvising Over Gospel Blues Changes in D

Chapter Fourteen
improvising over gospel changes in A

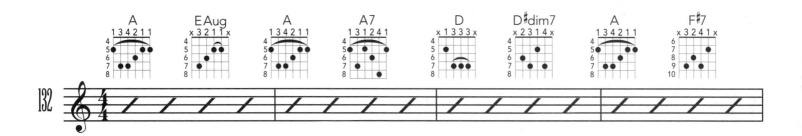

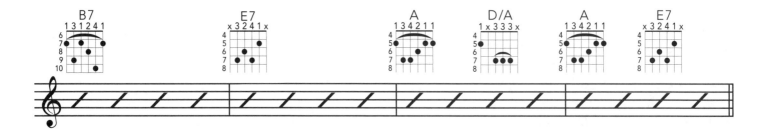

Study the gospel blues solo on page 83. The tempo is slower than the similar form in Chapter 13. Once again, you are playing over more chords than in the usual blues form. Notice the immediate transition from the A Major Pentatonic scale to the E Whole Tone scale (see page 94) to cover the E Augmented chord. Bar 2 uses the A Mixolydian mode as a strong push to the IV chord (D). Once again, play the chord tones for each chord in bars 3 through 6 followed by double-string ideas in the final two bars.

In this chapter, we'll investigate the style of Otis Rush. Along with Buddy Guy and Magic Sam, he helped bring the R&B and gospel feels to the blues in Chicago during the late 1950s. By adding different musical influences to the blues, he helped inspire many up-and-coming guitarists to new technical levels.

PHOTO • CLEVELAND STORRS\COURTESY OF STAR FILE, INC.

Otis Rush

Otis rush helped bring the R&B and gospel feels to the blues in Chicago during the late 1950s.

Eight-Bar Gospel Blues Solo in A

Chapter Fourteen: Improvising Over Gospel Changes in A

Licks in the Style of Otis Rush

Learn the following six licks in the style of Otis Rush and apply them to the eight-bar form.

This lick uses an A Major Pentatonic lick over the A chord followed by an E Major Pentatonic scale pattern over the E Augmented chord.

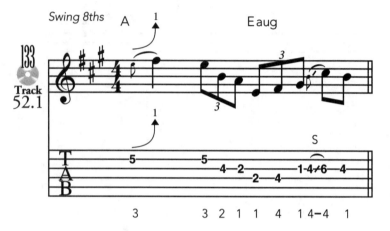

Here, the A Major Pentatonic scale moves smoothly over I (A) and III7 (F#7).

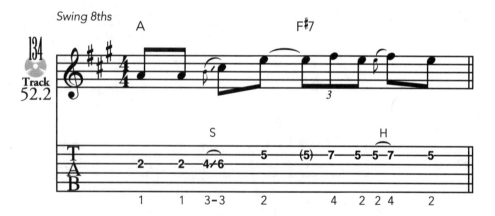

Here's a turnaround lick using the A Blues scale. The last two bars of the eight-bar format usually use the minor pentatonic scale (or blues scale) as a contrast to the heavy major pentatonic scale use throughout the first six bars.

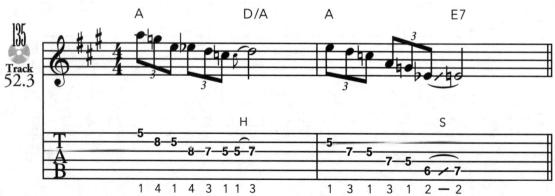

Blues Guitar for Adults

This is an A Major Pentatonic lick that ends on the ♭7 of the A7 chord (G).

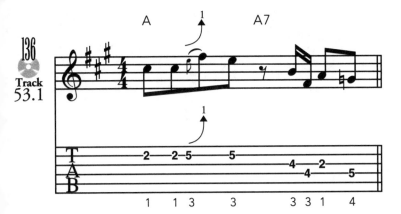

In this lick, the D Major Pentatonic scale is used over the D chord, followed by a D♯ Diminished 7 arpeggio (see page 95) over the D♯dim7 chord.

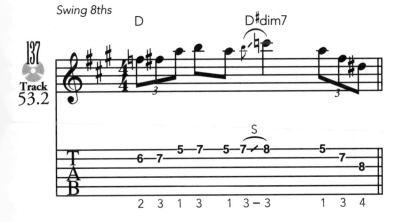

Here, the B Major Pentatonic scale is played over the II7 chord (B7) followed by the E Mixolydian mode with two cool half-step bends over the V chord (E7).

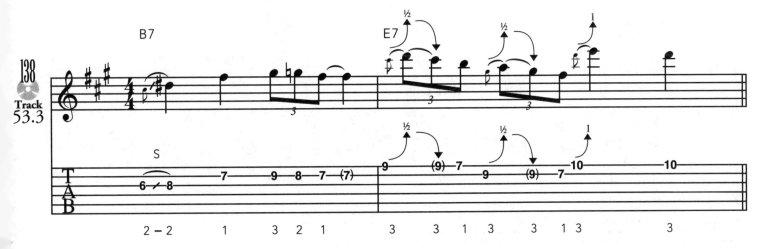

Chapter Fourteen: Improvising Over Gospel Changes in A

Chapter Fifteen
improvising over a blues in the style of "stormy monday"

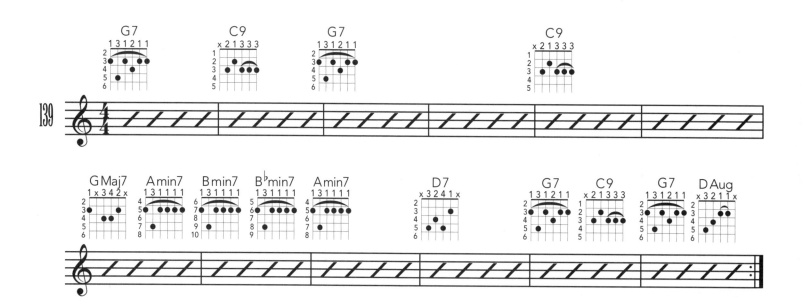

Study the solo over this classic blues format on page 87. Generally played at a slow tempo, the variety of chord changes gives you a chance to play some colorful licks. Bending into the chord tones of the IV chord (C9) adds immediate contrast to the standard G Minor Pentatonic scale licks. Bars 7 through 10 feature the unique chord pattern introduced by singer Bobby "Blue" Bland in the 1960s. The G Major Pentatonic scale works well over these chords because the changes move through the harmonized G Major scale. However, you can use arpeggios of the minor 7 chords in bars 8 and 9.

Let's take a look at the style of T-Bone Walker, the composer of "Stormy Monday." With his hollow-body guitar sound and outstanding musical technique, he imparted a melodic but bluesy flavor to his tunes. Originally from Texas, he developed the original Texas blues style and brought it to California in the 1940s and '50s. A flamboyant entertainer using a big band sound with a couple of horns, he added a new dimension to the blues.

T-Bone Walker

T-Bone Walker developed the original Texas blues style and brought it to California in the 1940s and '50s.

PHOTO • PICTORIAL/COURTESY OF STAR FILE, INC.

Twelve-Bar Stormy Solo in G

Chapter Fifteen: Improvising Over a Blues in the Style of "Stormy Monday"

Licks in the Style of T-Bone Walker

Learn the following six licks in the style of T-Bone Walker and apply them to the popular "Stormy Monday" format.

This typical lick in the style of T-Bone goes through the G Minor Pentatonic scale. The addition of the 9th tone (A) is what makes this lick work. Also, notice the resolution to the major 3rd (B) at the end.

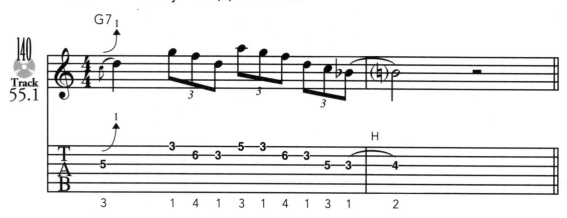

This G Blues scale lick on the lower strings also resolves to the 3rd on the final note.

This IV-chord lick moves from the G Minor Pentatonic to the G Major Pentatonic scale. It ends with a C9 arpeggio (see page 95).

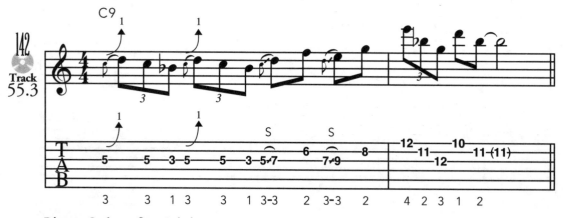

Blues Guitar for Adults

This C Mixolydian lick uses consecutive major 6th intervals followed by notes from the G Minor Pentatonic scale.

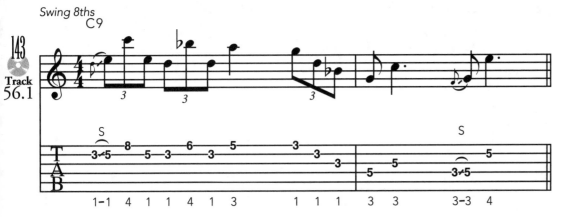

This great lick comes from the G Major Pentatonic scale and uses a bend into a tone of each chord.

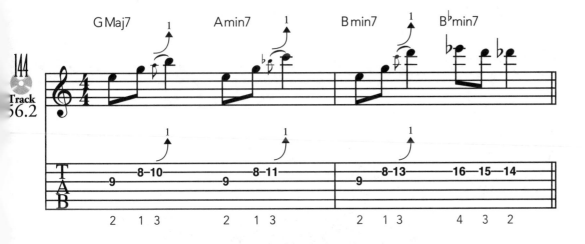

This lick is based on the G Major Pentatonic scale but the notes of the Amin7 chord are highlighted.

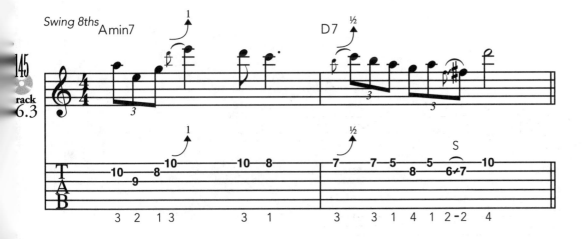

Chapter Fifteen: Improvising Over a Blues in the Style of "Stormy Monday"

Chapter Sixteen
improvising over alternate blues changes in B♭

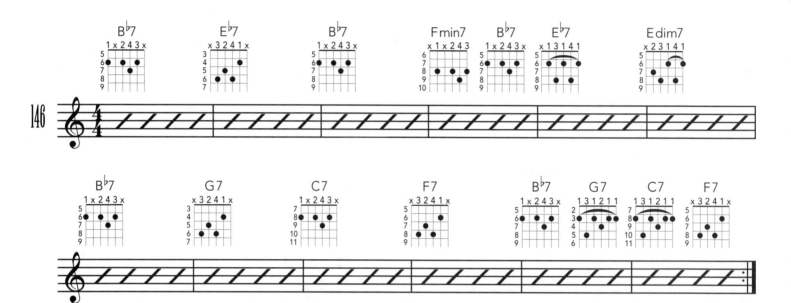

Study the solo over this medium tempo, jazz-blues form on page 91. In a classic blues style, players will occasionally add extra chord changes to the I–IV–V format. These can work well to add some variety as long as everyone in the band is on the same page, playing the same alternate changes. In this sample solo, the blues feel is intact, but watch for specific chord-tone licks over the added alternate chords.

In this chapter, we'll look at the style of Tiny Grimes. Because he could not afford to buy a six string guitar when he first started playing, he began using a four-string guitar (the top four strings). This became his trademark. If you listen to his recordings, particularly "Profoundly Blue," you can't tell the difference. He carried on the Charlie Christian tradition by using jazz and blues licks over a swing-blues feel. He began playing in the Washington D.C. area in the 1940s and made his mark in New York City with his own quartets and a three-year stint with the legendary pianist, Art Tatum.

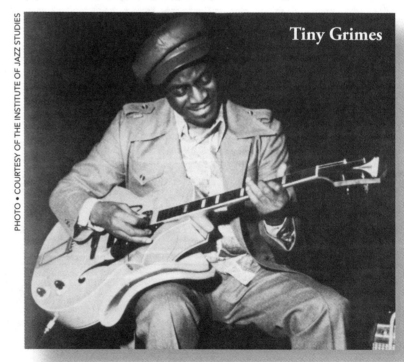

PHOTO • COURTESY OF THE INSTITUTE OF JAZZ STUDIES

Tiny Grimes

Tiny Grimes began playing in the Washington D.C. area in the 1940s. He made his mark in New York City with his own quartets and a three-year stint with the legendary pianist, Art Tatum.

Solo Over Alternate Twelve-Bar Blues Changes in B♭

Chapter Sixteen: Improvising Over Alternate Blues Changes in B♭

Licks in the Style of Tiny Grimes

Learn the following six licks in the style of Tiny Grimes and apply them to a blues with alternate changes.

This B♭ Blues scale lick resolves to the major 3rd (D) in bar 1 followed by an E♭7 arpeggio over the IV7 chord (E♭7) in bar 2.

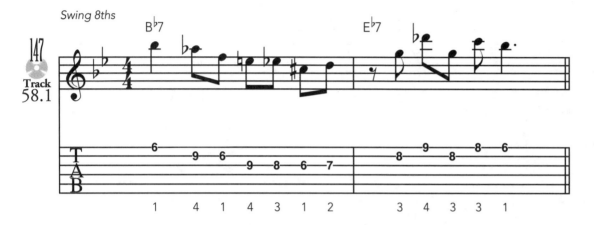

This B♭ Mixolydian lick works nicely over the third and fourth bars of the B♭ jazz-blues form.

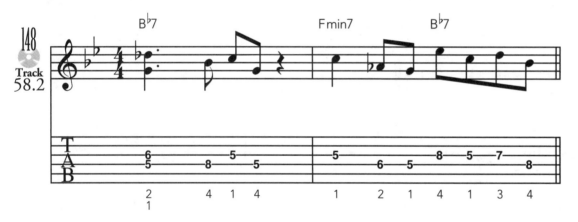

Over the IV7 chord (E♭7), move into the E♭ Major Pentatonic scale followed by an E Diminished 7 arpeggio over the Edim7 chord.

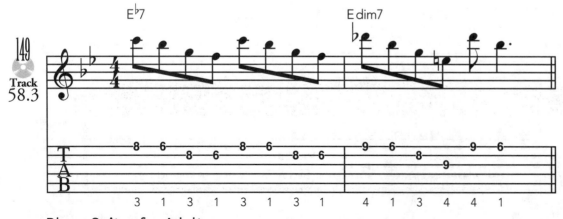

Blues Guitar for Adults

This one starts with a simple B♭ Major Pentatonic scale lick that is followed by a *chromatic* (using half steps) lick from the 3rd (B) to the 5th (D) over the G7 chord.

This is a C Major arpeggio lick with passing tones connecting to an F Major arpeggio with passing tones. It's this use of chromatic, non-chord tones that gives the lick its jazzy sound.

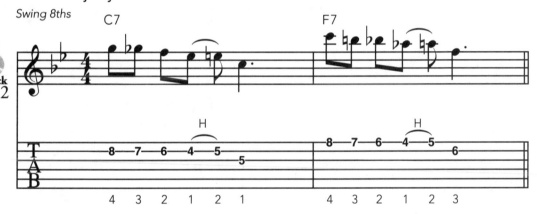

This chord-tone lick uses the tones of the B♭ and G7 chords and ends with a C Mixolydian lick in bar 2.

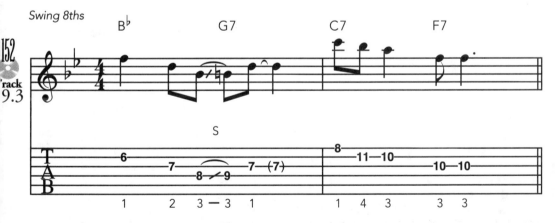

Congratulations!

You have completed *Blues Guitar for Adults.*
We hope you've enjoyed this no-nonsense look at the blues.
Don't stop now. Pick up your next instruction book today and keep learning.

Chapter Sixteen: Improvising Over Alternate Blues Changes in B♭

Scales

Here is a glossary of all the scales mentioned in this book. The roots are marked. If you ignore the open strings, all the patterns are fully transposable to any key by simply moving the root (marked in each diagram) to the root of the desired key.

A Blues Scale (A Minor Pentatonic)

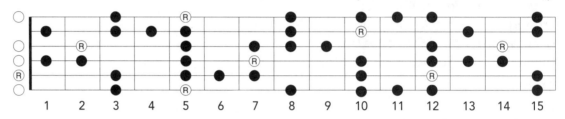

A Major Pentatonic Scale

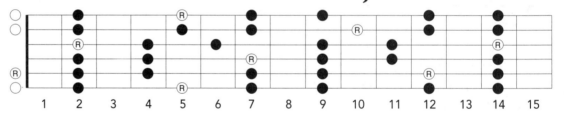

D Mixolydian Mode

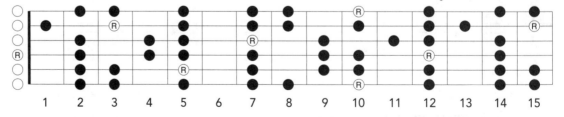

A Minor Scale

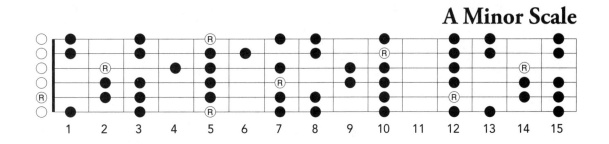

E Whole Tone Scale

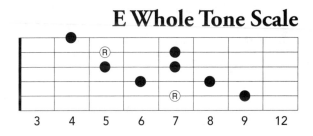

G# Diminished Scale

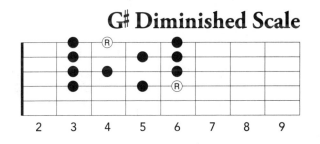

Arpeggios

As with the scales, these arpeggios are
fully transposable to any key.

A7 Arpeggio

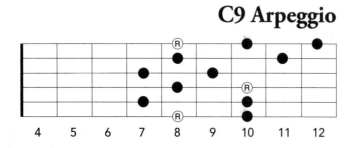

A Minor 7 Arpeggio

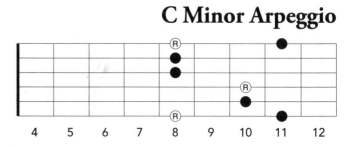

C9 Arpeggio

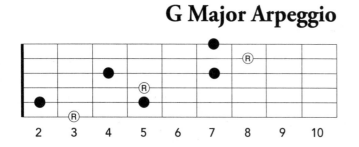

C Minor Arpeggio

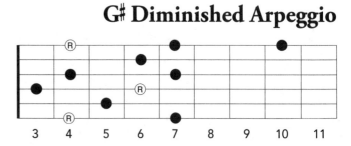

G Major Arpeggio

G# Diminished Arpeggio

E Minor 6 Arpeggio

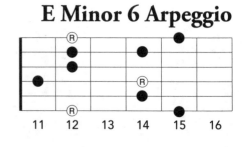